Marketing Action Plans

Outlines, Templates, and Guidelines for Gaining a Unique Competitive Edge

Morgan D. Rees

iUniverse, Inc.
New York   Bloomington

Marketing Action Plans
Outlines, Templates, and Guidelines for
Gaining a Unique Competitive Edge

iUniverse books may be ordered through booksellers or by contacting:

iUniverse
1663 Liberty Drive
Bloomington, IN 47403
www.iuniverse.com
1-800-Authors (1-800-288-4677)

Because of the dynamic nature of the Internet, any Web addresses or links contained in this book may have changed since publication and may no longer be valid.

ISBN: 978-1-4502-3733-8 (sc)
ISBN: 978-1-4502-3735-2 (dj)
ISBN: 978-1-4502-3734-5 (ebk)

Library of Congress Control Number: 2010908502

Printed in the United States of America

iUniverse rev. date: 7/13/2010

CONTENTS

INTRODUCTION

Just one hundred years ago, the majority of the nation worked for themselves or for a very small business, while the minority was employed by large businesses. For the past fifty years, however, this trend has reversed—now the majority work for giant corporations.

Remember when IBM dominated the entire global computer business? Do you recall when General Motors owned the global automobile market with over 60 percent market share? Kodak was synonymous with color film and held 90 percent marketing share. For decades you didn't say, "Make a photocopy," you said, "I'm going to make a Xerox." Now we have digital photography, and Hewlett Packard owns the color desktop printer market. Who in their right mind would have ever contemplated these pillars of industry would lose their standing?

We are in the midst of a work paradigm shift that is changing us from one way of doing business to another. It's a revolution. A transformation. A sort of metamorphosis. It didn't just occur; rather, it's driven by our changing times.

Workers are now being subcontracted for a specific initiative or project. This is indicative of the Silicon Valley business model; however, now globally. Now each one of us will not only have to have our own unique expertise of skill sets such as in engineering, product management, electrician, financial controller, etc., we will also have to be able to market ourselves as standalone services or companies. We now have to market ourselves against the other guy. *Marketing Action Plans* will expeditiously and painlessly bring you up to speed and provide you the outline, templates, and self-guidance to market yourself in the aggressive global village and give you the competitive edge.

Over my career I have read hundreds of marketing, branding, sales, and product management books. During that process, I usually highlight important areas with a yellow highlighter. Then, after finishing the book, I would circle back and type out all of the yellow highlighted areas. Regrettably, I have never been able fill more than a single page of information per book that I could actually use in my day-to-day job of marketing. In other words, my time was not being used efficiently, and the return on investment was low.

Marketing Action Plans is a 365-days-a-year resource tool. It's not the kind of book that sits on your bookshelf at home; rather, you should keep it with you at work at all times. Everything in this book is for real-world survival—individual documents, processes, procedures, and full plans.

All of us have had - or will have - a boss who demands a full public relations, marketing and/or online plan on his desk in less than a week. This is impossible to do from scratch; however, with *Marketing Action Plans* you will able to use 50 percent to 80 percent of each document and template included.

Simply insert your company name and products where asked. Yes, you will need some customization to fit your organization, but having a substantial part of your plan, layout, and content provided will permit you to do two things: focus on what is really important and meet your unrealistic deadlines.

Also, after decades of experience I can personally attest that having a process and check off forms dramatically speeds up your entire department. It will synchronize everyone in or outside of your marketing department. It usually takes years to develop a complete set of fully developed best practices lists. But now you, simply by reading this book, have virtually everything you need.

Enjoy your MAP to success.

Marketing Is the Navigator

Success Factors for the Emerging Technology Company

Marketing is the Navigator

Venture capitalists have a saying, "If you don't know where you are going, any road will get you there." Many start-ups are founded by technical innovators, whose vision is primarily focused on the technical capabilities of their products. However, the "better mousetrap" may not succeed in the marketplace. For the emerging company introducing its high-tech products, marketing should be an equal partner in guiding the conceptual thinking, market requirements, direction setting, product development, and product launches—the essentials that determine the ultimate success of the start-up and its product offerings. The marketing organization plays the role of navigator—advising on the customer-focused objectives, the processes and methods for execution, and the best course for developing and launching products on time and within budget.

At emerging technology companies, the marketing organization can play a key role in establishing and steering the company's directions. Marketing can ensure that a company's technical vision is balanced by an understanding of the wants and needs of its target customers, for example, the CIOs and network managers of Fortune 1,000 enterprises.

Investors are often instrumental in guiding technology entrepreneurs to focus on marketing and rely on marketing-driven processes. The typical management team at a start-up company is more enamored with embellishing the bells and whistles of their technology than understanding and addressing the requirements of their target customers. I am impressed when it is demonstrated how integrated marketing is in the core fabric of the company and when implemented marketing-driven methodologies keep a company focused and on track.

Before new product development gets under way, the marketing organization should be tasked with answering fundamental questions such as:

- What are we selling?
- What is the product?
- Who will we sell it to (and how do we get them)?
- Why will they buy it (and why won't they buy it)?
- What is the competition?

This focus on marketing can enable an emerging company to diversify its product portfolio by leveraging its core competencies. The marketing team can identify market requirements for additional products based on the core technology but with differentiating functions that meet specialized requirements. Because the underlying technology is the same for all products, the company can shorten the development time for new products.

CRITICAL SUCCESS FACTORS

At an emerging company, marketing can drive critical success factors, including:

- Ensuring unified corporate wide commitment on vision, strategies, and plan
- Building tools to ensure the success of the sales organization
- Managing the product development process
- Gaining intimate knowledge of the market and evolving customer needs
- Achieving, sustaining, and managing perception of product performance

The marketing plan for each product incorporates elements including alignment with the company mission, value proposition, marketing fundamentals, market segment profiles, market size, market share objectives, competitive landscape, product delivery requirements, product road map, marketing tactics, sales strategy, and resource plans. The cumulative mix of these elements defines a multidimensional matrix that drives the company's sales goals, time lines, budgets, and staffing.

The integration of the marketing perspective into all aspects of the planning and execution process forges an externally oriented, customer-driven consciousness. The marketing-driven company leverages the perceptions of its visionary technologists to develop a vision that ultimately wins the hearts and minds of its customers. This customer focus permeates product requirements documents, product road maps, engineering plans, and customer support requirements, sales presentations, beta product releases, and ongoing product development. A marvelous transformation occurs when the "customer becomes everything." Every department and every member of the company begins to share a unified commitment to the company's vision, a common strategy, and integrated plans.

A Balance of Progress and Perfection

Management's role is to identify and clearly state objectives, associate those objectives with achievable metrics, track progress towards those objectives, identify obstacles in real-time, and engage a rapid decision-making process that overcomes those obstacles. Rather than increasing bureaucracy with ever-increasing levels of approval, the company should implement "lightweight" processes that people can understand and use. By continually emphasizing the company's focus on the customer, the marketing organization helps to achieve a balance between progress—"we've got to ship the product on time"—and perfection—"we've got to fix every bug."

The marketing organization can help to achieve the balance between progress and perfection by honing the emerging company's ability to execute its core competencies and identifying strategic partnerships that extend product capabilities and related solutions. For example, if the company's engineering team primarily consists of software developers, but the market requires an appliance-level solution that integrates software and hardware, hardware elements can be licensed from best-of-breed partners.

Understanding the trade-offs related to issues such as underlying hardware architectures is a critical element of the perfection versus progress equation. Some start-ups spend millions of dollars developing application-specific integrated circuits (ASICs) that provide high performance but are expensive to modify and difficult to enhance. Others have understood, however, that Moore's Law ensures the ever-increasing performance of Intel processors will enable them to maintain state-of-the-industry performance. This saves millions of dollars in R&D and enables the company to rapidly develop new software capabilities independent of the restrictions associated with ASIC-based systems.

Marketing can steer the company's product development by championing flagship customers, the initial users of a new product, or strategic partners whose satisfaction measures progress in real-world terms and signifies an acceptable level of perfection. Working through product requirements and needed refinements with these key customers and partners helps to ensure that a product's feature set, performance level, and price point meets or exceeds customer needs and provides a compelling differentiation to competitive products.

Ultimately, marketing is not an afterthought to the process of innovation; it is the essential catalyst that takes technology from the concepts of technologists to the reality of customer acceptance. With marketing organization as navigator, the emerging company knows where it is going, chooses the best road to get there, and arrives on time to the welcome of an ever-increasing legion of satisfied customers.

# # # #

A Running Start

Whether you are a freshly promoted marketing decision-maker or a new marketing leadership hire, you only have a single chance to make a first impression. This is an awkward period. Senior management is expecting you to immediately produce an action plan without knowing much about—or anything about—your company or its products. You want the honeymoon time to create a beautiful annual marketing plan that will impress everyone and put your fingerprint on the company. The reality is you are never given the luxury of time, as a thirty- sixty- ninety-day marketing plan is expected first.

How to use this chapter's materials: The following thirty- sixty- ninety-day marketing plan provides you the opportunity to distribute a fast plan for your first months on the job. This will placate senior management into permitting you to publish the level of quality marketing plan you want. Without quickly publishing a thirty- sixty- ninety-day marketing plan, you will be under intense pressures every inch of the way.

Included in this chapter:
* The thirty-, sixty-, ninety-day plan

THE THIRTY-, SIXTY-, NINETY-DAY PLAN

For the first thirty days joining your company you should conduct an overall market survey with the employees, sales' required tools for success, marketing, executive management's vision and channel needs. Below are the key elements that would be integrated into the overall launch campaign.

- Advertising
  - Radio
  - Trade and business publications
  - Newspapers
  - Outdoor media
  - Directory listings
  - Direct marketing
  - Postal and e-mail marketing
  - Trade Shows and conferences
  - Seminars, Webinars
  - Viral marketing

- Product collateral
  - White papers (print, Web)
  - Datasheets (print, Web)
  - Brochures (print, Web)
  - Corporate and product slide presentations
  - Videos (on Web, too)
  - Demos (including Web)
  - Customer case studies (print, Web)
  - Newsletters (print, e-mail)
  - Application guide
  - Gifts and promotions
  - Logo items (clothing, cups, hats, trinkets, posters, etc.)

- Web site presence and promotional offers
  - Collateral as cited above
  - Special product discounts/offers

- Cross-link promotions
- Banners and logos on other sites

- Web site presence and promotional offers
  - Special product discounts/offers
  - Cross-link promotions
  - Banners and logos on other sites

- Web site planning elements
  - The first element is planning
  - The second element is content
  - The third element is design
  - The fourth element is involvement
  - The fifth element is production
  - The sixth element is follow-up
  - The seventh element is promotional
  - The eighth element is maintenance

OUTLINE:

ONLINE / DIRECT E-MAIL CAMPAIGN

- Text e-mail blasts (monthly): list rental for an example from IDG
- The rental list includes: reseller of computer/network products, ISP, people who are purchasing Internet/ Intranet products, people who are planning to purchase Internet/ Intranet products and people who are planning to install relevant network platforms.
- HTML postcard send to our own internal list (biweekly)
- Online advertising and lead generation through ISP market that includes: banners, newsletters, discussion list, and text links
- Online banners: Hosting Tech, TechWeb, The Web Hosting Industry Review, XSPsite.net, ISPortal.com, E-Commerce Times, Network World, and Channel Web.
- Online newsletters: ISPortal daily news, XSPsite.net
- Online discussion list sponsorship: ISP-CEO, ISP-WebHosting, ISP-Collocation, ISP-E-commerce and ISP-Load Balancing

- Online text links: E-Commerce Times

WEB SITE PRESENCE AND ONLINE MARKETING

- Online marketing will only work if our company understands marketing
- Online marketing means a lot more than having a Web site
- Online marketing is only a small percent of all marketing

The insight is that we must continue marketing with traditional media. The Web site needs marketing.

The options are many:
- Multiple links to other sites
- Banners leading to our site
- Search engines directing browsers to our site
- Chat conferences heralding our site
- Recommendations of our site by Internet powers
- E-mailing to parties demonstrably interested in learning about the topics covered on our site
- Mentioning our site in our e-mail signature
- Versions of our press kit to publish our site online
- Connecting with as many other online entities as possible

All can contribute to making our site part of the online community, an Internet landmark to our prospects, a not-to-be-missed feature of the Web.

Promote the site on:
- Corporate, product, and classified ads
- Stationery
- Business cards
- Signs
- Brochures and other collateral
- Packages
- Business forms
- Gift certificates
- Reprints of PR articles
- Radio
- Direct marketing campaigns

Promotions will lure them to our site; killer content will cause them to make return trips. Pay extra close attention to how easy it is to find our company. Does our site appear near the top in all the search engines? Is it on the first page of any classified search? Can visitors directly access the data they need rather than having to navigate through many unnecessary pages?

Prospects really want: safety, convenience, speed, service, information, personal attention, and good values.

- What is the immediate, short-term goal of our Web site?
- What specific action do we want visitors to take?
- What are our specific objectives for the long term?
- Who do we want to visit our site?
- What solutions or benefits can we offer to these visitors?
- What data should our site provide to achieve our primary goal?
- What information can we provide to encourage them to act right now?
- What questions do we get asked the most on the telephone?
- What questions and comments do we hear most at trade shows?
- What data should our site provide to achieve our secondary goal?
- Where does our target audience look for infractions?
- What may be the reasons we don't sell as much as we'd like to?
- Who is our most astute competitor?
- Does our competitor have a Web site?
- What are ways we can distinguish ourselves from our competitors?
- How important is price to our target audience?
- Global PR program
- Product and partner press releases
- Executive interviews, profiles, and presentations (U.S., Europe)
- Analyst briefings

- Product reviews
- Customer stories in media

PRESS RELEASES

- Quarterly financial releases
- ˙Strategic business/partnerships

ALL MEDIA RELATIONS' FOCAL POINT

- Product review program
- Create written brand voice
- Keeper of written strategic messaging

COMMUNICATION TOOLS

- Collateral
- Ensure our product messaging is focused and consistent in all published materials and mirrors the message architecture of the platform
- Support PR as needed with materials to fulfill press needs, which will integrate PR messages with marcom messages
- Prepare creative materials to support trade shows and other events and contribute to their success by developing pieces that convey the message and promote the brand
- Ensure that all co-marketing opportunities leverage and support the brand
- Develop training materials to support sales strategy
- How to sell our products, solutions, and applications in the market today
- How to overcome common objections
- How to use company marketing and sales programs and resources such as field engineers
- How to sell against competitors

WEB SITES

- Continue to upgrade the product launch site with article reprints, success stories, etc. as more information becomes available

- Add movement and visual interest: video, Flash animation and interactive demonstrations
- Maintain responsiveness to forum questions by responding within twenty-four hours
- Create special trade show landing sites with loads of information on partners and what will be presented at the show
- Develop plan to create an online community/user group

ENDORSEMENTS

- Analysts
- Industry experts
- Key market watchers
- Partners
- Customers
- Strategic partner support
- Press releases
- Customer stories
- Other media features
- Trade shows and conferences

LEAD GENERATION PLAN

- Direct mail (no charge)
- If have merchandise credits with publications that we advertise with that can be put towards direct mail names.
- E-mail (approximately $5,000 for five thousand names)
- Most publications are about the same price for the e-mail. It varies a little depending on search criteria. May want to try purchasing from numerous magazine lists.
- Webcast sponsorship ($7,000)
- IT World will provide leads from their on-demand Webcast. You can sponsor a series as you choose to help target your efforts.

WHITE PAPER HOSTING ($4,000 / MONTH)

Recommend getting a contract for six months or so and swapping out white papers as they get written. Price drops to approximately $3,600 a month per white paper if commit to six months of hosting.

PRODUCT SHOWCASES

Overview
In a series of large cities we will conduct product showcases

PURPOSE:

Train VAR community
Obtain and leverage VAR customer database
Exploit as a sales tool to close new VAR business
What is our status?

SALES TRAINING

At the beginning of 20__, we will institute a sales training program to enhance the selling skills of the sales channels. The product familiarization workshops will be in three phases due to the large amount of distribution outlets and geography.

FIRST PHASE OF TRAINING

First will be the U.S. direct and representative/dealer sales force. This training uses an integrated approach to provide product information and advanced selling concepts. The training will be conducted at each of our four regional offices. The training workshop will be at each branch office for three days.

SECOND PHASE OF TRAINING

A national tour of twenty major cities is planned to train as many dealers as possible. Each city visit will be two days long due to the magnitude of attendees.

THIRD PHASE OF TRAINING

Another national tour of twenty major cities is planned to train as many resellers as possible. Each city visit will be two days long due to the magnitude of attendees.

INTERNAL ANNOUNCEMENT PACKAGE

- To the sales force

- To other personnel
- Manufacturing
- R&D

PRESENTATION TO SALES FORCE

- PowerPoint slide presentation
- Other presentation material

INVENTORY PLANNING

- Phase in/phase out

SALES HANDBOOK

- Cover letter
- Product strategy
- Features
- Competitive evaluation—product sourcing and product testing

CUSTOMER SERVICE ENGINEER BRIEFING

POST INTRODUCTION EVENTS

- Sales tracking
- Promotions

MARKETING PLAN—TELEMARKETING

END USER LEAD GENERATION ESTIMATED COSTS

(Outsource to telemarketing subcontractor)

1. Purchase database
2. Select and load data
3. Set up telemarketing screens and management reports
4. Develop script
5. Train operators
6. Operation hours
7. Management fee

Reseller Recruitment

1. Research and input checkpoint resellers
2. Research list availability for resellers selling products within your industry.
3. List selection (set up charge)
4. Purchase agreed list
5. Load data
6. Set up telemarketing screens and management reports
7. Develop script (in conjunction with company)
8. Train operators 300
9. Operation hours (based on speaking to 400 DCM)

Branding and Advertising

Having a brand identity—a positive, unifying theme that comes to the mind of customers, prospects, and passive bystanders when they hear your company's name—is the heart of any marketing plan. Still, many companies either ignore it or don't understand it, publishing haphazard, disconnected messaging that makes it difficult for people to understand what the company is about.

Huge advertising agencies / brand houses can charge up to a million dollars just to create a unified communications corporate branding plan. Done correctly, it is worth every penny.

How to use this chapter's materials: Read "The Power of the Brand" to build a better understanding of just how crucial branding is. From there it's important to bring your thought leaders together to develop a direction—so get your CEO/president, VP of sales, CFO, VP marketing, etc into a single room and agree on the questions in the Executive Questionnaire. This would be a huge step forward.

The remaining templates will help you develop and execute your branding strategy.

Included in this chapter:
- The Power of the Brand
- Templates
  - Executive Questionnaire
  - Positioning Outline
  - A Unified Communications Approach

- Brand Strategy and Launch Plan

How to use the advertising materials embedding in the branding chapter: "Advertising Components and Reasoning" explains the major components of advertising and why they're important. Use the Creative Inventory Assets template to help organize your creative tools and pieces—and to give you a heads-up on what you're missing.

Included at the end of the branding chapter:
• Advertising Components and Reasoning
• Templates

THE POWER OF THE BRAND

The power of the brand to influence purchasing decisions is often overlooked in the market for complex business technology products. However, a strong brand represents key purchasing criteria for products. Particularly in large enterprises that require business executives to approve the procurement decisions of their technical subordinates, the swaying power of the brand is often a key determining factor in the purchasing decision.

Companies like Cisco, Microsoft, Intel, and Apple understand the power of the brand and invest millions of dollars to build and sustain their brands. Emerging companies, however, tend to focus the lion's share of their attention and resources on perfecting the technical capabilities and inner-workings of their products, building the better mousetrap, as the saying goes, and neglecting to pay sufficient attention to how their brand appears in the marketplace. Such companies often pay the price for brand neglect only after they have convinced a technical evaluator at a prospective account of the technical superiority of their product. They then discover that the purchasing decision requires the approval of a CIO or management committee that is not especially familiar with the product category or related technology.

"I've never heard of them" is a buzz-killing refrain that can make a salesman wince and create an insurmountable barrier to entry that even the biggest price discount cannot overcome. This is why the emerging company should balance its technical zeal with a comparable focus on creating its brand. The company's marketing team plays a key role in achieving this balance, but ultimately brand building becomes a responsibility shared by everyone in the company. Even the most marketing-averse technology executive will come to embrace the bottom-line value of the brand to enable the company to sell more products at higher prices.

WHAT IS A BRAND?

What is a brand? A brand is composed of multiple elements. It starts with a promise that you deliver on consistently. It evolves as a valued partnership between you and the customer. It grows into a community of passionate users of the company's products or services. It becomes a crucial part of your customer's identity. In other words, customers identify with the brand. They think, "This brand speaks for me. It is an illustration of what I stand for."

Consider Nike. It used to be "Nike: Just Do it," accompanied by the "swoosh" marquee. Today, everyone knows that "Just Do It" refers to Nike. The same for the "swoosh."

Strong brands such as Nike, Sunkist, McDonald's, Coca-Cola, Kodak, Yahoo!, eBay, and others succeed because their organizations focus on presenting clear and consistent brand images. Branding is more than words; it requires consistent execution at every level of the organization. All employees must understand the brand and live and breathe its values in every interaction with the customer.

THE GOALS OF AN EFFECTIVE BRAND STRATEGY

The emerging company must consider a number of elements in executing a brand strategy to ensure that:

- People know what to expect when they see the brand.
- People respond positively and emotionally to the brand. What is the feeling that the brand will produce?
- The "message" or "essence" of the brand impinges on every single contact that occurs between the product or company representative and any customer or potential customer in the world.
- The brand's message simply and clearly differentiates it from competing brands.

Effective brand positioning is rooted in customer values, clearly differentiates your brand from competitive brands, and articulates the underlying strategy and rationale for pricing, promotion, product development, distribution, and service. Good branding insulates you from competitors, increases customer loyalty, makes loyal customers less price-sensitive during the crucial purchase process, and becomes a financial asset that is particularly vital to the success of stock offerings, mergers and acquisitions, strategic partnerships, or other company financial activities.

Branding occurs across a range of activities that can include:

- Advertising in trade and business publications, in newspapers; on radio and television; in outdoor media such as billboards, bus and cab banners, and airport posters; and in-flight promotions
- Directory listings, direct marketing, postal and e-mail marketing, trade shows and conferences, seminars, Webinars, viral marketing, and permission marketing
- Product collateral, including white papers, data sheets, brochures, slide and Web-based presentations, videos, case studies, newsletters, posters, and gifts and promotions, including "chotskies" such as clothing, cups, hats, key chains, etc.
- Web site presence and promotional offers, including special product discounts and offers, cross-link promotions with other Web sites, and banners and logos on others sites
- Public relations activities, including product and partner press releases, executive interviews, profiles and speaking presentations at conferences, seminars and other industry events, analyst briefings, product reviews, customer stories placed in business, trade, and vertical industry publications, endorsements, references from industry influencers, market watchers, partners and customers, strategic partner activities, including joint press releases, joint marketing activities and customer stories and presence at trade shows and conferences.

THE POWER OF PERSUASION

The power of newspapers is news. The power of magazines is credibility. The power of radio is intimacy. The power of direct mail is urgency. The power of telemarketing is rapport. The power of brochures is the ability to give details. The power of television is the ability to demonstrate. The power of the Internet is interactivity. The power of billboards is to remind. Ultimately, the power of advertising is to persuade a potential customer to reach out to declare their interest in receiving more information or a sales contact.

For the purposes of this branding discussion, "advertising" is any paid mass media attempt to persuade. As with any mass communication, it can be perceived as either a positive influence that helps us make informed decisions and occasionally amuse us, or, alternatively, as a negative influence that creates media clutter and nags us to buy products.

So why advertise? At the simplest denominator, it reaches people in places and at times that media coverage generated through public relations does not. It also supplements media coverage and, in some cases, helps to actually generate coverage. It also creates buzz by creating an image and turning a company and its products into familiar names. Done well, advertising builds awareness, generates demand, and produces sales leads.

Advertising requires a commitment to repetition, with messages being conveyed across diverse media as well as within a specific genre. Establishing majority market share for technology products is not only about getting there first—it is also communicating that you are there with the greatest value-added offering.

The ability of advertising to reach a customer who would otherwise never become aware of your company or product must be complemented and reinforced by the customer's experience from the moment they respond to the ad by clicking on your Web site to the packaging, user interface, documentation, and customer support that surround and accompany your product. Even the signs in your parking lot and the appearance of your corporate offices contribute to the customer's experience of your brand.

Good branding translates into the buzz created by word of mouth as satisfied customers spread the word about their favorable experience with your company and your products. The powerful brand indeed becomes an extension of the customer's own identity. Marketers and entrepreneurs have a great deal to gain from exploring what customers are saying about their products. While your technologists remain intent on building the better mousetrap, a complementary focus on building the company's brand will help to ensure that customers beat a path to your door.

# # # #

Templates (How to Use)

Welcome to the first section of the book that contains templates and workflow guidelines. Throughout the entire book are compilations that tap into areas that range from marketing, public relations, investor relations, inside sales and trade shows to quality assurance and customer retention. The templates and workflow guidelines are placed within the appropriate subject matter.

Simply insert your company name and products where asked. You will need some customization to fit your organization, but having a substantial part of your plan, layout, and content provided will permit you to do two things: focus on what is really important and meet your unrealistic deadlines.

The templates and processes that follow throughout the entire book will include:

- Executive questionnaire
- Positioning outline
- Public relations templates, (plan, process)
- Trade show management and execution (PR plan and seminar checklist)
- President's trade show introduction letters
- Internal trade show survival guide
- Investor relations process flow
- Inside sales process
- Collateral status at a glance
- Inside sales process, policies, and procedures/workflows (including qualified lead hand-off and conversion
  - Inside sales—baseline script
- Marcom team process flow
- Marketing materials order form for sales
- Quality assurance strategy templates
  - Sieve overview
- Customer retention templates
  - Frequent users club
  - Volume incentive program
  - Value-added resellers' templates

- Co-op plan recommendations
- Cooperative advertising pact
- Value-added reseller agreement and more.

Efficiency control is the task of increasing the productivity of such marketing activities as selling, advertising, sales promotions, and distribution.

Templates and processes provide fundamental tools and concepts for delivering optimal results in the world of scant budgets and human resources. These templates and processes enable us to do more with less.

Executive Questionnaire

Name:

1. How would you briefly describe what (insert your company here) does? (Elevator pitch)
    A:

2. What would you say is the company vision?
    A:

3. What do you think are (insert your company here) core strengths?
    A:

4. What do you think are (insert your company here) main weaknesses?
    A:

5. How would you describe the (insert your company here) value proposition to a prospective customer?
    A:

6. What three main customer problems does (insert your company here) address?
    A:

7. Who are your top three competitors?
    A:

For Sales Executives:

8. Who are your five most important customers? How much revenue did they produce, and what specifically led them to select (insert your company here) products?
    A:

9. Tell us about some customer "wins" in the past six months. Why did they buy?
    A:

Positioning Outlines

Research

The analysts said …

Summary of competitors' coverage:

- Briefs pertaining to competitors' acquisitions and how that affects their market position and future standing.
- Competitors appear to have very strong brand recognition and a highly positive profile among these analyst firms.

Media Audit

Media Audit
Reflects perception, not reality

From seven targets
- Few industry experts
- Eight questions

Top of mind awareness (unaided)
When you think of companies that do what you do, which company comes to mind first?

Industry leadership (ID)
In your opinion, is there one company that is paving the way for this market or stands out in your mind as the recognized leader?

Your markets
For each of the companies that you have heard of, how do you see them fitting into the market? In other words, what do you think is their main business?

Brand personality (known)
For those companies that you have heard of, what is your impression of them or what words would you associate with them?

Brand personality (unknown)
For those companies that you have not heard of, what is your impression of them or what words would you associate with them?
Media audit implications

COMPETITOR POSITIONING

Positioning is:
A clear articulation of:
- The problems your brand solves for its primary target audience(s)
- The compelling benefits of your products and services
- The differentiation of your products/services/solutions from those of your competitors
- Believable, supportable messages based on core competencies—bulletproof

Positioning is not:
- A mission statement (internal—what you do today)
- A vision statement (internal—what you'll do tomorrow)
- A tag line (external—your brand promise)

Objectives for positioning
- To elicit input from company thought leaders
- Rule #1: Say it now or forever hold your peace.
- To encourage open, objective discussion
- Rule #2: It is far better to be hurt by the truth today than the market tomorrow.
- To reach high-level consensus re: breakthrough corporate positioning and key messages
- Rule #3: Keep it at 50,000 feet.

POSITIONING STATEMENT

Your brand essence is an emotional reaction to your brand. It's what your company does ... what you're known for ... and why customers prefer your brand. It is often used as the basis for a tagline in visual communications, and it's at the core of brand loyalty.

- Coca Cola is the authentic soft drink.
- Nike empowers you to achieve.
- GE improves the quality of your life.
- Chevrolet trucks are indestructible.

Your company's brand essence

The brand personality statement helps to develop the tone and manner of communications. By assigning human qualities to companies, it becomes easier to define your brand experience. This is especially important when dealing with visual communications media, as these qualities should carry over to your brand's look and feel.

A UNIFIED COMMUNICATIONS APPROACH

- Goal: present a clearer, more cohesive vision of (insert your company here) which includes a (insert industry here) position and strategy.
- Continue existing selected major brand promotions (specify key brand carriers)
- Integrate selected product and technology messages into two related, high-level (insert industry here) branding efforts (create brand clusters)

COMMUNICATIONS TODAY

- Multiple nonrelated messages lead to lack of critical mass and momentum
- no cohesive vision of (insert your company here)
- no stated (insert industry here) strategy (or direction into a digital (insert industry here) future)
- We burden our publics to
- sort out, analyze, and sum our various messages
- form a perception of (insert your company here) that matches our desire

The effect on (insert your company here) brand image and equity

- Our public's perceptions of (insert your company here) today depend on them adding up the messages and, in essence, self-creating the corporate image
- Will it be coherent, focused, integrated?
- more likely: multiple, nonintegrated messages = unclear perception of (insert your company here)' strategy, focus, technology advantages, and "inherent product value"

STRUCTURAL VERSUS CLUSTER BRANDING

- Structural brand
  - sending messages out of many separate P&L

  - separate budgets, separate messages

  - scattered segmentation of technologies and products

- Cluster branding
  - combining of messages across businesses to frame a market-sensible view

  - corporate budget, corporate message

  - arbitrary, focused segmentation of technologies and products

Brand clusters and key brand carriers

- Brand cluster: claim leadership to (insert industry here)
- Key brand carriers: selected major brand activities used differently to more clearly define (insert your company here)
- New brand clusters plus key brand carriers form a core view of the business
- these can ride below a continuing corporate image campaign, or
- these can, in and of themselves, represent the corporate campaign

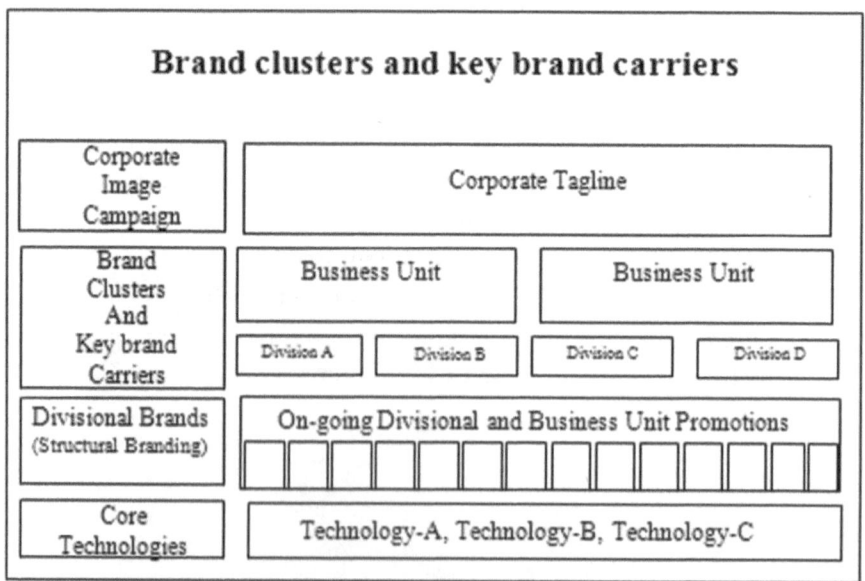

Benefits of clusters branding

- Easier for (insert your company here)' publics to position the company in a positive, coherent way
- The whole appears greater than the sum of the parts
- aids expression of a uniform personality
- creates a means to better measure company brand equity
- allows shaping and shifting of messages to suit market conditions from corporate view
- Leverages greater proportion of communication spending from selected divisions

Is there a (insert your company here) (insert industry here) position?

- Extensive analysis completed (insert industry here) and applications
- Vectors identified: some resources we have, some we must acquire—in any case, we must move!
- After constructing a position, we must create messages and deliver them
- cluster branding can help, without sacrificing other existing brand momentum

COMPETITIVE (INSERT INDUSTRY HERE) POSITIONS

Insert industry-A companies	Insert industry-B companies
- A1	- B1
- A2	- B2
- A3	- B3

Brand Strategy and Launch Plan

Insert company name here

Brand Strategy and Launch Plan

First Draft - Date

Insert product picture here

(Merely insert your company name and products where asked. You will need some customization to fit your organization; however, a substantial part of your brand strategy and launch plan, layout, and content are provided.)

CONTENTS

I. Introduction

(Insert company name here) challenges the status quo of the (insert industry here) industry, long mired in single-function solutions that were difficult to integrate and deploy. (Insert company name here) ignores the traditional and ordinary approaches to the market and embraces the visionary maxim set forth by CEO/President (insert CEO's name here), "Empower the customer with integration, flexibility, and simplicity."

These key elements of the (insert company name here) brand are evident in every aspect of the (insert company name here) product line and every interaction with the customer. They are manifested in the company's product goals, which are to deliver:

These key elements of the (insert company name here) brand are evident in every aspect of the (insert company name here) product line and every interaction with the customer. They are manifested in the company's product goals, which are to deliver:

- The most user-friendly user interface
- The most configurable solution
- The most rapid and flexible (insert feature here)
- The most powerful (insert feature here) platform

As (insert company name here) extends its product line to include not only (insert feature) solutions, but also (insert feature) solutions for the enterprise, the company will continue to deliver on its key promises to the customer:

Integration, flexibility, and simplicity.

II. The Power of the Brand

What Is a Brand?

- A promise that you deliver on consistently
- A valued partnership between you and the customer
- A "community" of passionate users of the company's products or services

- A crucial part of your *customer's* identity. In other words, customers identify with the brand. They think: "this brand speaks for me. It's an illustration of what I stand for."

Consider Nike. It used to be "Nike: Just Do It," accompanied by the "swoosh" marquee. Today, everyone knows that "Just Do It" refers to Nike. The same for the "swoosh."

Strong brands such as Nike, Sunkist, McDonald's, Coca-Cola, Kodak, Yahoo, eBay, and others succeed because their organizations focus on presenting clear and consistent brand images. Branding is more than words; it requires consistent execution at every level of the organization. All employees must understand the brand, and live and breathe its values in every interaction with the customer.

THE BASIC GOALS OF AN EFFECTIVE BRAND STRATEGY

- Ensure that people know what to expect when they see the brand.
- Ensure that people respond positively and emotionally to the brand. What is the feeling that the brand will produce?
- Ensure that the "message" or "essence" of the brand impinges on every single contact that occurs between the product or company representative and any customer or potential customer in the world.
- Ensure that the brand's message simply and clearly differentiates it from competing brands.

EFFECTIVE BRAND POSITIONING:

- Is rooted in customer values.
- Clearly differentiates your brand from competitive brands.
- Articulates the underlying strategy and rationale for pricing, promotion, product development, distribution, and service.

BENEFITS OF GOOD BRANDING

- Insulates you from competitors
- Increases customer loyalty

- Makes loyal customers less price-sensitive during crucial purchase process
- Brand becomes a financial asset.

III. THE (INSERT COMPANY NAME HERE) BRAND

The corporate name refers to (insert company name meaning) that the company offers its customers, as well as to the company's clustering technology.

Company Name (here)
Tagline (here)

Tagline
The corporate tagline positions (insert company name here) as a provider of easy-to-use, high-performance technology solutions for improving the performance of the products.

"Company Man" Figure (Mascot Figure)
The "Company Man" figure represents the confidence and mastery of the product user who deploys (insert company name and tagline here)

The (insert company name here) Icons
The icons represent the essential functions that (insert company name here) products integrate.

Customer Values That the Brand Conveys
- The need to be in cool, confident control of operations
- The need for powerful, integrated, flexible, and easy-to-use "tools" to manage and operations
- The need to reduce the complexity, cost and risk of

_____

IV. The (Insert product name)— Extending the (insert company name) Brand

(Insert company name) has identified a significant new opportunity that leverages its core technology to deliver a third-generation (insert vertical sector here) product, to be called (insert product name).

The Need for (insert key feature/solution)

"Insert industry analyst quote here"
—Analyst name, Analyst with analyst firm.

Some companies are so concerned about (insert industry: security or protection or consumer electronics etc.) that it's the area of operations slated for the largest spending increase this year. __percent of companies with revenue up to $100 million, __ percent of businesses with revenue between $100 million and $1 billion, and 15 percent of companies with $1 billion or more in revenue are making _____ their key focus in the months ahead. Most of that investment will be spent fortifying _____, say __ percent of small, __ percent of midsize, and __ percent of large companies.

Beyond first-generation _____ and dedicated _____ are today's primary second-generation means of establishing _____. Companies such as (insert competitor-A), (insert competitor-B), (insert competitor-C) and (insert competitor-D) and others are pioneering the market for third-generation _____. (insert company name) can leverage the high interest in (insert industry) to position itself as a premium supplier in the emerging third-generation space.

To address this market opportunity, (insert product name) is (insert company name) second product line, coming after its initial (insert current product name) product line.

(Insert product name) Marketing Objectives

- Launch (insert product name) to position (insert company name) as a dominant player in the highly visible and growing market for third-generation (insert industry) solutions

- Deploy (insert product name) in (insert either small business or midsize or enterprise business), enabling the cross-selling of our current (insert existing current product line here).

TARGET CUSTOMER

_____ of corporate _____ and _____

CUSTOMER NEED

Deliver (insert key feature/solution) to trusted partners and employees anytime, anywhere

PRODUCT DIFFERENTIATORS

- Nondisruptive (insert type of application such as wireless or network) integration
- The most trustworthy and user-friendly (insert type of application such as wireless or network) platform
- Continue list ....
- _____ and _____ capabilities
- The ultimate (insert feature) in the (insert industry category) industry

THE PROBLEMS WITH COMPETING PRODUCTS

- (Insert competitions product)
- expensive
- Require complex setup and operations, interoperability between sites, and specialized software
- Proprietary appliances
- Lack the level of technology and performance that (insert product name) offers

V. THE (INSERT PRODUCT NAME) BRAND

By emphasizing information (insert industry here) and operational vigilance, the (insert product name) brand fits dynamically into the (insert company name) brand strategy of empowering (user title here) with confidence and mastery over their (insert either small business or midsize or enterprise business) sector.

Tagline

The product tagline positions the (insert product name) as an (insert either small business or midsize or enterprise business) product that provides (insert feature here) access to (insert either small business or midsize or enterprise business) business information—anytime, anywhere.

The (insert product name) Look and Feel

The (insert product name) brand is reinforced through a brand identity including a unique look and feel that is consistent with the existing (insert company name) brand identity.

Customer Values that the (insert product name) Brand Conveys

- Cool, confident control of (insert either small business or midsize or enterprise business) access
- Assure employees and partners of secure information exchange
- Extend and make more flexible the boundaries of (insert either small business or midsize or enterprise business) workplace.

(Insert product name) Positioning Overview

Today's (insert industry product category here) solutions are primarily focused on (inset type of optimization) optimization and (inset product's function) without really identifying, limiting, or (insert function). This makes high-performance products such as the (insert company's existing products name) the ideal solution for traditional applications.

With the migration of applications to the (Web or replace with industry), employees, vendors, customers, and strategic partners of (insert either small business or midsize or enterprise business) organizations can now fully enjoy the benefits of easy, remote access of (insert benefit or function). This access, however, cannot be managed by current (insert appliance product here) tools alone. After all, while tools that are optimized for performance are powerful, they do not effectively address (insert either small business or midsize or enterprise business) (insert industry here) needs.

(Insert company name) presents a new class of (insert what your product delivers, does, or solves) specifically designed with the needs of the (insert either small business or midsize or enterprise business) in mind. Optimized for (insert industry), the (insert product name) enables corporate (insert user title here) to effectively deliver _____ to _____ without requiring complex and proprietary (select either hardware or software). Equally important, the (insert product name) transparently handles (insert feature or solution here) traditionally associated with _____ and _____.

Based on a (insert industry here) platform (your company name here), (insert company name here) product is the first _____, end-to-end _____ solution that allows for _____, user-friendly interface and integrates proven (insert your company name here) technologies such as (company name here) OS™, (insert product feature here) and (insert product feature here).

VI. (INSERT INDUSTRY HERE) MARKET OVERVIEW

THE NEW EXTENDED (INSERT EITHER SMALL BUSINESS OR MIDSIZE OR ENTERPRISE BUSINESS)

The extended (insert either small business or midsize or enterprise business) has become a major source of competitive advantage for companies as they extend the virtual boundary of their operations to leverage economy of scale and scope to compete effectively in the twenty-first century. The new extended (insert either small business or midsize or enterprise business) encompasses:

- Strategic partners
- Suppliers
- Customers
- Geographically disperse remote offices (domestic and international)

- Traveling employees
- Remote workers

THE NEED FOR (INSERT INDUSTRY HERE) SOLUTIONS

The key enabler for the extended/virtual (insert either small business or midsize or enterprise business) is a _____ solution that would enable all the key players within the extended/virtual (insert either small business or midsize or enterprise business) to exchange information in a secure and timely manner. Information is critical to the success of the extended/virtual (insert either small business or midsize or enterprise business) because it drives decision-making, which leads to productivity improvement, cost competitiveness, customer satisfaction, revenue enhancement, and eventually market leadership.

Traditionally (insert either small business or midsize or enterprise business) have provided (insert industry here) to corporate information through the deployment of legacy technologies such as _____, _____, and _____ which are well-suited to linking the offices of individual companies, but are ill-suited to the needs of organizations that, in increasing numbers, need to exchange critical (insert item: data, music, etc) with business partners as they implement (insert type of strategy) strategies.

In addition, as markets are becoming increasingly global, many companies are faced with unacceptably high costs whenever _____ crosses international boundaries. At the same time, as more workers _____ and _____, traditional _____ services have become too expensive and cumbersome to serve the needs of the increasingly dispersed and mobile workforce. These trends have put strains on traditional (insert industry) infrastructures.

_____ has emerged and has been adopted by (insert either small business or midsize or enterprise business) as an alternative/substitute technology which leverages the _____ to provide _____ to company information in a timely and cost-effective manner to anyone, anytime, and anywhere.

THE (INSERT PRODUCT NAME) OPPORTUNITY

The (insert product name) is a (insert what product does here) platform that utilizes (insert company name)' high-performance _____ and _____ technology to deliver an attractive complement to current (insert current industry solution here)'s. (Insert product name) offers benefits to _____ providers and (insert either small business or midsize or enterprise business) that include:

- Provide anytime and anywhere _____ using standard _____
- Simplify set up, operation, and maintenance of _____ solutions
- Lower total cost of ownership versus (insert existing solution) deployment
- Minimize the time requirement to enable partners and employees to be able to access internal resources
- Eliminate many of the interoperability issues faced by (insert current solution here) deployment

CURRENT ALTERNATIVES FOR (INSERT SOLUTION YOU ARE PROVIDING)

The customer pain point that (insert product name) addresses is the need for a product that enables (insert either small business or midsize or enterprise business) to provide their customers, employees, partners, and suppliers with (insert your solution here) to critical business information. (Your solution here) involves _____ and _____ users before allowing them to _____. It also requires appropriate _____ support, using _____ mechanisms that do not require proprietary software or hardware.

Alternative technologies that address this market include _____, _____, _____, _____, Web _____, and specialized _____ devices. However, (insert current solution here) is the most popular mechanism and the fastest growing solution for _____.

Even though (insert current solution here) has significant market acceptance, it has three main deployment issues that make it vulnerable and lead to customer dissatisfaction and defection.

1. A major shortcoming is the interoperability of (current solution) across multiple (current solution) vendors. For

example, a business with multiple partners that deploy (current solution) solutions from various vendors cannot cross-communicate. At issue is _____, the key management _____ protocol used in (current solution) are so complex and stand in the way of interoperability. There is an _____ effort to standardize this so that (current solution here) solutions are interoperable. It is probably a year to two away from coming to fruition, if it does at all.

2. Management is another problem and gets worse as the size of the customer base grows. (Current solution) needs a proprietary _____ requiring special configuration that includes among other things, modifications to _____ so that clients can reach (insert technical device) on the inside.

3. (Current solution) typically gives _____. This could enable additional operational cost and complexity.

(INSERT PRODUCT NAME) MARKET REQUIREMENTS (APPENDIX A)

VII. COMPETITIVE INFORMATION

Several companies are offering ____ _____ products. (insert competitor A) and (insert competitor B) are perceived as the primary competitors.

(Insert competitor A)   Format: (hardware or software and solution)
Product: (insert what does it do)
Positioning: (insert how product is positioned)

(Insert competitor B)   Format: (hardware or software and solution)
Product: (insert what does it do)
Positioning: (insert how product is positioned)

(Insert competitor C)   Format: (hardware or software and solution)
Product: (insert what does it do)
Positioning: (insert how product is positioned)

(Insert competitor D)   Format: (hardware or software and solution)
Product: (insert what does it do)
Positioning: (insert how product is positioned)

(Insert competitor E)   Format: (hardware or software and solution)
Product: (insert what does it do)
Positioning: (insert how product is positioned)

(Insert competitor F)   Format: (hardware or software and solution)
Product: (insert what does it do)
Positioning: (insert how product is positioned)

Competitive Matrix	(Insert Company Name)	Insert Competitor A	Insert Competitor B
	(Insert Product Name)	(Insert Product Name)	(Insert Product Name)
Solution A			
Feature	**Yes**	Yes	**No**
Feature	**Yes**	Yes	Yes
Feature	**Yes**	Yes	**No**
Solution B			
Feature	**Yes**	Yes	Yes
Feature	**Yes**	Yes	Yes
Feature	**Yes**	Yes	Yes
Solution C			
Feature	**Yes**	Yes	Yes
Feature	**Yes**	Yes	Yes
Feature	**Yes**	Yes	Yes
Solution D			
Feature	**Yes**	Yes	Yes
Feature	**Yes**	Yes	Yes
Feature	**Yes**	**No**	**No**
Solution E			
Feature	**Yes**	Yes	**No**
Feature	**Yes**	**No**	**No**
Feature	**Yes**	Yes	**No**

The Purchasing Process

The purchase of (insert appropriate industry) solutions for an enterprise is a complex process involving several members of the management staff, all of whom are involved in the evaluation, recommendation, and final approval. Thus, the brand strategy must appeal to both the technical and economic decision-makers in the enterprise. The diagram shows the complexity of the purchasing process.

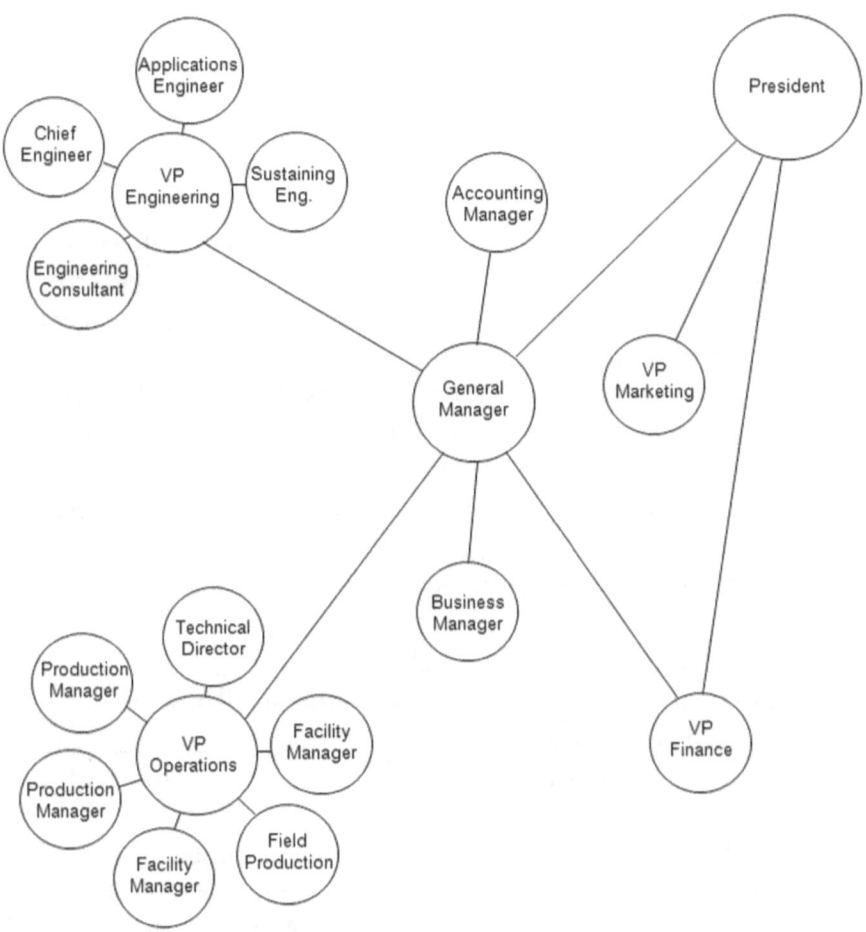

VIII. (Insert product name here) Sales Pitch

There is a clear trend towards moving information to (example: a Web-based format) (insert your solution here) that companies such as (examples: Siebel, PeopleSoft, and Oracle) (insert your competitor companies here) have made extremely clear. As this happens, the requirements to offer your users _____ follows the anytime-anywhere _____ mantra.

The key issue to this difficulty is the requirement of proprietary _____ tools to enable _____. More often than not, they require use of complex _____ that require that the _____ infrastructure between the _____ and your _____ be able to accommodate—something that will never work for 100 percent of your users.

Matters only get more complex as the number of_____ required by your users increases. An (insert either small business or midsize or enterprise business) can easily have dozens of _____ for different departments that are _____ under different areas.

Bringing up all of the potential (if not present) problems that plague your users (and by extension, plague you) is only fair if a solution can be had. Introducing the (insert product name). The all singing and all dancing solution to allowing true (insert product solution here), (insert product solution here), and (insert product solution here).

The (insert product name) offers these solutions by leveraging what your users already have on their _____.

Getting the Basics Right

Starting with the (insert product name) OS™ foundation, the (insert product name) offers lightning-fast _____. A feature necessary to support what often feels like a huge, ever-growing (insert either small business or midsize or enterprise business). Capable of _____ new _____ transactions per second or users, the (insert product name) isn't a slouch.

In addition to its _____ performance, the (insert product name) sports an impressive _____ and _____ technology that allows for the extremely fast handling of _____. Whether the system is under _____ or is simply taking on your entire (insert either small business or midsize or enterprise business) needs, the (insert product name) will exceed performance expectations.

No matter how well a single system can perform, catastrophe can always strike. Power plugs get pulled, cabling drops don't get wired correctly, switches fail, or, most dangerous of all, junior employees get involved. In these cases, it is prudent to have a backup system available and the (insert product name) can make that happen. With support for _____gathering up to __ systems, you cannot only achieve impressive duplicity, but incredible scalability as well.

USER INTERFACE

As the (insert industry here) tools we use to solve our problems have become increasingly complex, so have their user interfaces. This is unfortunate because so many of the knobs and dials that are necessary to manage a device have reasonable defaults that could make the process so much easier.

The (insert product name) addresses this head-on with the (insert your company here) (insert user interface name here), an extremely intuitive Web interface. Designed from the ground up, users everywhere can take a deep breath at the thought that they no longer need to deal with yet another training course for yet another language.

The true pinnacle of the (insert product name)'s user interface is the (insert interface name here). Like a pilot's instrument panel, the (insert interface name here) allows your users an at-a-glance view of what's going on inside the (insert product name). Automatically updated at regular intervals, your customers can simply leave an open window on their desktop to see what's going on.

BUILDING IT RIGHT

All of Silicon Valley's most brilliant minds can design the most robust, secure, high performance system, but it only takes one mistake. Understanding that the physical threat is just as significant, the (insert product name) sports an impressive industrial design that looks as good as it works.

HOW IT WORKS

Let's assume for the moment that you've got _____ that you want to _____. Let's look at the steps a request takes when going through the (insert product name).

Step 1: The Initial Request
The user opens up _____

Step 2: The Login
Once the user has _____

Step 3: Getting Content
With the Web page showing what content the user can _____. The user now views the requested content; the (insert product name) *goes on to the next step.*

Step 4: Moving the Content between _____ fetches the content from the _____ etc., etc., and then passes it all back to _____.

A UNIFIED VIEW OF THE WORLD

One of the significant benefits of the (insert product name) is its ability to give a uniform _____ your services.

From the perspective of needing to train users, this is a godsend. Rather than needing to inform some users of some _____ and other users of other _____, only further complicating the matter by the fact that they are accessed differently from whether you are at the corporate office or on the road, you can now simply tell them, "Go here." Where "here" is the (insert product name). The (insert product name) provides a simplified single point of entry that works for all users, all the time. This unified view of the world is accomplished by the union of the (insert product name)'s mapping function features.

IX: THE (INSERT PRODUCT NAME HERE) LAUNCH

The (insert product name) is launching in conjunction with the _____ trade show. The brand launch campaign incorporates several of the following key elements:

- **Advertising**
  - Radio
  - Trade and business publications
  - Newspapers
  - Outdoor media (billboards, bus and cab banners, airport poster, etc.)
  - Directory listings
  - Direct marketing
    - Postal and e-mail marketing
    - Trade shows and conferences
    - Seminars, Webinars
    - Viral marketing

- **Product Collateral**
  - White papers (print, Web)
  - Data sheets (print, Web)
  - Brochures (print, Web)
  - Slide presentations
  - Videos (on Web, too)
  - Customer case studies (print, Web)
  - Newsletters (print, e-mail)
  - Gifts and promotions
  - Logo items (clothing, cups, hats, trinkets, posters, etc.)

- **Web Site Presence and Promotional Offers**
  - Special product discounts/offers
  - Cross-link promotions
  - Banners and logos on other sites

- **Global PR Program**
  - Product and partner press releases
  - Executive interviews, profiles, and presentations (U.S., Europe)
  - Analyst briefings
  - Product reviews
  - Customer stories in media

- **Endorsements**
  - Analysts
  - Industry experts
  - Key market watchers
  - Partners
  - Customers

- **Strategic Partner Support**
  - Press releases
  - Customer stories
  - Other media features
  - Trade shows and conferences

X. ADVERTISING COMPONENTS AND WHY

For the purposes of this plan, "advertising" is any paid mass media attempt to persuade. As with any mass communication, it can be perceived one of two ways:

- As a positive influence, helping us make informed decisions and amuse us as well
- As a negative influence, convincing us to buy products and creating media clutter

So why advertise? At the simplest denominator, it reaches people in places that media coverage does not. It also supplements media coverage, and, in some cases, it has been argued that advertising helps to actually generate coverage. It also creates buzz. It helps to make an image, product, and brand a household name.

MEDIA POWER

- The power of newspapers is news
- The power of magazines is credibility
- The power of radio is intimacy
- The power of direct mail is urgency
- The power of telemarketing is rapport
- The power of brochures is the ability to give details
- The power of television is the ability to demonstrate
- The power of Internet is interactivity
- The power of billboards is to remind

Advertising, however, requires a commitment to repetition, with messages being conveyed across diverse media, as well as within a specific genre. Establishing majority market share in networking products is not only about getting there first—it's also about communicating that you are there with the greatest value-add offering, first.

Across all media, (insert company name) will continue to track effectiveness of media with unique extension URLs tagged onto advertising. The URLs also enable users to follow up for more information.

RADIO

Radio is bigger, better, and more effective than ever. The cost of radio is exceedingly low when you consider how many members of our target audience that we can reach repeatedly; no other medium allows for such one-to-one intimacy. In addition, the targeted audience has most likely made the radio station a part of their identity, and they give credence to what the station announcers say.

In parallel with outdoor media strategy, (insert company name here) is using radio as direct marketing, making an offer and requiring a toll-free call for the buyer to accept it.

Technology products should target technology radio programs and/or celebrities, since their demographics include network savvy and early technology adapters, which is a good fit. In the ever-changing world, radio celebrities frequently move. Use the following list as a starting point and as a rough reference. If you contact a specific radio station and the person mentioned is no longer there, simply ask for their replacement.

Bill Bennett—Network
Clear Channel Online—LA
Colin Cowherd—Network
Craig Allen—WCBS AM NY
Dennis Prager—Network
Glenn Beck—Network
Kim Komando—Network
Laura Ingraham—Network
Leo Laporte—KFI LA
Michael Medved—Network
Mike Gallagher—Network
Michael Savage—Network
Neal Boortz—Network
Sirius Satellite Radio

UK RADIO
Talk Sport
Smooth FM (London and NW)
LBC FM
Gaydar Radio
OneWord Radio

Radio campaigns should air during rush hour, as well as on radio live online. The radio spots clearly state what action is required and how to take that action. Our radio call to action is to visit our www.companyWebsite.com.

Repetition is paramount in making any radio commercial effective: repetition of your company name, repetition of the prime benefit or offer, and repetition of the commercial. The radio spot is being aired several times a day, five-days a week, for at least three weeks.

TRADE AND BUSINESS PUBLICATIONS

(Insert company name) brand marketing is strategizing and executing a "series approach" advertising plan that is running in core business as well as trade publications. The ad plan is multitiered, the first tier building brand awareness for (insert company name) with a hint at the product offering that is yet to come. The next tier focuses on the benefits and problems solved by our products. The (insert company name) background message then shifts to a secondary position. As advertising ramps up, dilution of the message must be avoided.

There is a high crossover audience between the readers of the core books and those of other vertical publications. However, there was a sharp downturn in mainstream publication advertising, with a shift towards Internet and technology business publications. Despite the loss in advertising market share, however, PC-genre magazines still lead in advertising dollars spent.

Research indicates that 61 present of Americans read magazines from front to back, an inordinately high readership for a relatively tiny investment.

(Insert company name)' campaign has been evaluated for its effectiveness in business publications, including *Red Herring*, *Fortune*, *Forbes*, and *Time* or *Business Week*. To reach engineering management, placement in *EE Times* and *Electronic Business News* has been considered as well. Across all publications, the minimum measuring bar for considering placement was audience-purchasing influence at least at 50 percent, as well as companion online publication advertising opportunities.

Advertising efforts are currently focusing in the trade press publications with the most extensive reach, including (list your industry publications, such as *Network World*, *Network Computing*, *Network Magazine*, *PC Magazine*, *CRN*, and *VAR Business*). (Insert product name) advertising includes an advertorial placement in (industry focused magazine), where the (insert product name) story is conveyed and highlights (insert company name)' executive management.

(Insert company name) advertising efforts include:

1. Scouting regional editions of national magazines
2. Running (insert product name) ads in one regional edition one time only—we'll leverage the reprints
3. Ordering reprints of our ad, each emblazoned with credibility building "as advertised in *Time* magazine" (or other publications)

LOCAL, REGIONAL AND NATIONAL NEWSPAPERS

As budget allows, we will launch a local, regional, and national newspaper campaign to complement our other advertising. As with the trade publications, this campaign will include companion online opportunities. Due to the timelines of newspaper advertising, we will use this medium for conveying a strong, immediate call to action. Our local newspaper advertising will target those cities that are key technology hotspots, with a minimum of two drops per city.

(Insert company name) is running an ad in the (insert local newspaper publisher) "We are hiring," to highlight to appropriate parties that we are in a strong position in the industry and marketplace.

DIRECTORY LISTINGS

A plethora of online and printed industry directories and catalogues exist, in which the (insert company name) and (insert product name) brands should be listed. Often, the listings are free of charge and simply need to be researched, applied for, and maintained. Paid listings are also available and can be evaluated on a case-by-case basis, depending on factors such as traffic, proven impressions, and sell-through. We will research these opportunities and ensure that (insert company name) and (insert product name) are correctly represented in as many of these vehicles as possible.

DIRECT MARKETING

Our current customer base is a valuable resource, since it costs one-sixth as much to sell something to an existing customer as it does to sell to a new customer. Therefore, a primary goal is to stay in close touch with our existing customer base, as well as to extend our reach to targeted prospects. Direct marketing (postal and e-mail), based on targeted mailing lists, is the most accurate way to do this.

(Insert company name) direct mail activities include:

- Weekly electronic direct mail campaigns to targeted VAR list, Salesforce.com list, and analyst seminar lists
- Providing partners with electronic direct mail templates
- Researching in-house direct mail campaign to VAR mailing list and *PC Magazine* rental list

How Direct Marketing Supports Sales

The average electronic industry sales call costs approximately $1,000+ per visit. The average sales visit needed to close a sale is 5.1 sales calls. A 5.1 average visit and a $1,000 cost per visit makes the average cost to close a sale over $5,000.

The following charts represent anecdotal conclusions. They are difficult to quantify since the results are dependent on numerous variables, such as the quality of the direct mail piece itself, the company sending them, the product, and competitive pricing. I drew from personal experience, observations, and opinions.

The curve below illustrates that when a message is introduced; the average person remembers only one half after the first day and after thirty days forgets 90 percent of the message.

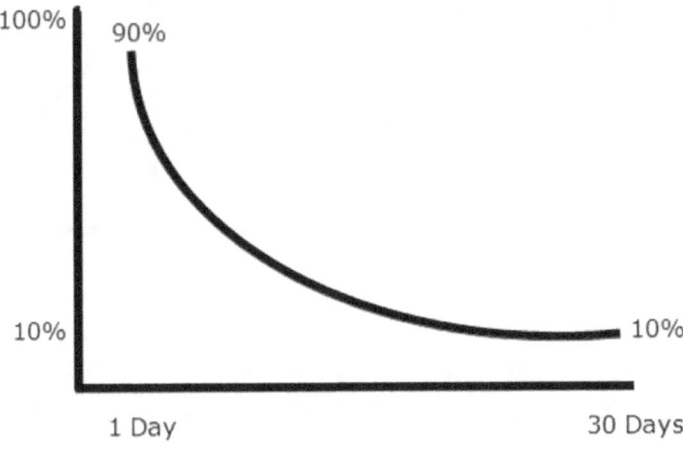

HUMAN TENDENCY TO FORGET CURVE

When a message is introduced, the average person remembers only one half after the first day and after thirty days forgets 90 percent of the message.

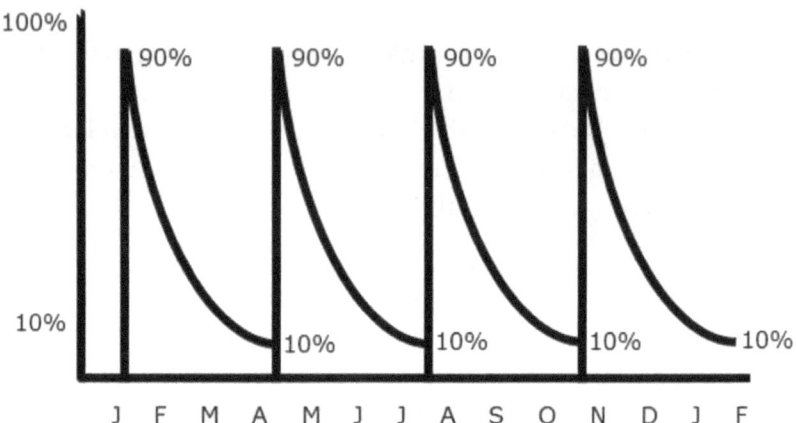

Because a salesperson cannot be everywhere all the time, the salesperson should be supported with direct mail, catalogs, publicity and advertising programs. Doing this retention will increase to 20 percent or more.

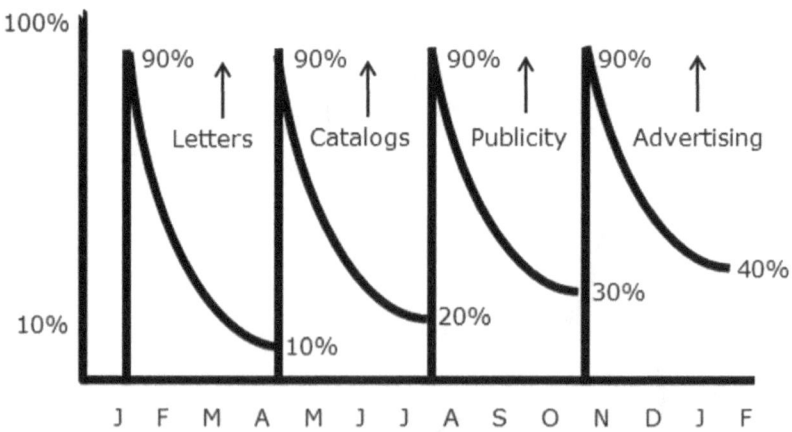

While viral e-mail relies on an interactive community to spread news to like members, subscription marketing relies on a single piece of data to deliver marketing messages. Typically, this single point relates to an expressed interest or "subscription." A marketer would attempt to match interest categories against the target audience in order to develop a list of recipients.

Database marketing relies on detailed information about members of a database to target marketing messages. Typically, the database contains profile information on each member, including demographic and psychographic data, interest information, and preferences. Marketers are then able to access this data and build a list of optimal recipients to receive a particular message, matching the qualities of the audience they are seeking against the profiles of members of the database.

Clearly, the more detailed database provides more flexibility and a more powerful marketing option, frequently yielding higher response rates and a better ROI.

Permission-based or opt-in marketing means that each and every recipient in a given database has made a conscious decision to accept marketing materials.

With today's rising costs in making sales calls, (insert company name) is sending out a campaign of electronic direct mail to raise visibility of (insert company name) and introduce (insert product name) to target audiences, highlight its key benefits, and reinforce the (insert product name) and (insert company name) brand attitudes and values.

At product launch time, companies tend to send out an overt sales message with a discount of some type attached. After the initial barrage of e-mail, snail mail, and sometimes telemarketing, the company is either quiet until the next launch or in the interest of maintaining an ongoing customer relationship. Essentially, the difference between the follow-on pieces being considered either useful or a nuisance is the inclusion of useful material.

To continue to develop customer relationships throughout the year:

- (Insert company name) will execute a direct mail and direct e-mail campaign newsletter developed for follow-on relationship management.
- Direct mail (postal): Three drop DM campaign, with two rounds of e-mail in between each drop. The lower-cost e-mail

campaign will convey similar messaging to harmonize with and reinforce the postal pieces.

SEMINARS AND WEBINARS

We should also conduct seminars and additional training for our customers and prospects. The results of such programs will increase customers, gain new strategic partnerships, and improve (insert product name) customer satisfaction.

TRADE SHOWS AND CONFERENCES

Industry seminar trade shows such as (insert trade show event here) provide a focal point for (insert industry here)-industry professionals and offer a cost-effective opportunity to reach a broad cross-section of the industry, including influential buyers who may be difficult to target with other promotions.

UPCOMING EVENTS

- (Insert strategic partner) Expo
- Infosec
- SUPERCOMM
- Networld Interop
- Breakaway Xchange (VAR oriented event)

VIRAL MARKETING

The Internet remains a gold mine for marketers. However, banner advertising has become increasingly less effective, as consumers face a bombardment of banner messaging when they try to focus on their primary goal, which is to find relevant information. As a result, click-through rates are steadily decreasing.

Viral marketing, however, provides another way to leverage the Internet. Although usually classified under the umbrella of direct marketing, a successful viral campaign will usually reach a far greater audience than the target individuals for whom the program was launched. As its name suggests, viral marketing causes the message to replicate and spread from one recipient to the next, sometimes unpredictably.

Viral marketing is not to be confused with targeted HTML-based e-mail campaigns, which are really an extension of direct mail. Hotmail began as an excellent example of viral e-mail. The link that accompanied each Hotmail message invited users to set up their own Hotmail account. Each happy user of Hotmail automatically invited friends and associates to join, simply by sending them e-mail.

We will consider ways to exploit viral marketing in spreading word about the (insert product name) brand and drawing Web users to the (insert company name) Web site. Marketing is considering giving out (insert company name here) user interface in order to gain fast market acceptance, broad traction, and establish the company as an emerging leader in the space.

FOLLOW-UP ON ADVERTISING AND DIRECT MARKETING LEADS

To manage the follow-up, we are using a documented lead fulfillment process via our inside sales/telemarketing organization. Marketing implemented, with the help of IT, and a tracking system.

XI. PRODUCT COLLATERAL

In addition to the deliverables for the advertising and PR campaigns, we are developing a wide range of product collateral, including

- White papers
- Data sheets (print, Web)
- Brochures (print, Web)
- Corporate and product slide presentations
- Demos (including Web)
- Customer case studies (print, Web)
- Newsletters (print, e-mail)
- Promotional gifts
- Application guide
- Web site presence and promotional offers
- Collateral as cited above
- Special product discounts/offers
- Cross-link promotions
- Banners and logos on other sites

XII. Web Site Presence and Promotions

- Online marketing will only work if (insert company name) understands marketing
- Online marketing means a lot more than having a Web site
- Online marketing is only a small percent of all marketing

The insight is that we must continue marketing with traditional media. The (insert company name) Web site needs marketing.

The options are many:

- Multiple links to other sites
- Banners leading to our site
- Search engines directing browsers to our site
- Chat conferences heralding our site
- Recommendations of our site by Internet powers
- E-mailing to parties demonstrably interested in learning about the topics covered on our site
- Mentioning our site in our e-mail signature
- Versions of our press kit to publish our site online
- Connecting with as many other online entities as possible

All can contribute to making our site part of the online community, an Internet landmark to our prospects, a not-to-be-missed feature of the Web.

Promote the site on:

- Corporate, product, and classified ads
- Stationery
- Business cards
- Signs
- Brochures and other collateral
- Packages
- Business forms
- Gift certificates
- Reprints of PR articles
- Radio

- Direct marketing campaigns

Promotions will lure them to our site; killer content will cause them to make return trips. Pay extra close attention to how easy it is to find (insert company name). Does our site appear near the top in all the search engines? Is it on the first page of any classified search? Can visitors directly access the data they need rather than having to navigate through many unnecessary pages?

Prospects really want: safety, convenience, speed, service, information, personal attention, and good values.

- What is the immediate, short-term goal of our Web site?
- What specific action do we want visitors to take?
- What are our specific objectives for the long term?
- Who do we want to visit our site?
- What solutions or benefits can we offer to these visitors?
- What data should our site provide to achieve our primary goal?
- What information can we provide to encourage them to act right now?
- What questions do we get asked the most on the telephone?
- What questions and comments do we hear most at trade shows?
- What data should our site provide to achieve our secondary goal?
- Where does our target audience look for infractions?
- What may be the reasons we don't sell as much as we'd like to?
- Who is our most astute competitor?
- Do our competitors have a Web site?
- What are ways we can distinguish ourselves from our competitors?
- How important is price to our target audience?

XIII. Launch Activities

(Insert company name) is promoting its entry into the (insert industry name) market through its sponsorship of the (insert analyst firm name) Conference, its presence at the (insert strategic partner name) Executive Summit, and its exhibit at the (insert trade show event name) (insert city, state here) trade show. The _-city tour is an opportunity to set additional briefings with press and analysts in each city. Included in the promotion is a European press tour in (insert country) and (insert country).

Analysts Event Name Here

Day, month date at the _____ (insert hotel name here), (insert city here)
Day, month date at the _____ (insert hotel name here), (insert city here)
Day, month date at the _____ (insert hotel name here), (insert city here)

The (insert analyst firm name) conference is highlighted by (insert your CEO/president name here) panel participation: The (insert event name here): How, When & Why with other executives from (insert company A, insert company B and insert company C) moderated by _____ _____, (insert analyst name) senior analyst of (insert industries here) solutions and services. Concurrently, (insert your CEO/president name here) is introducing the (insert product name) to press and analysts, in conjunction with his travels to (insert city, state here), (insert city, state here), and (insert city, state here). (See target press/analysts in public relations section below.)

Seminar Description

We know you know (insert industry name here) is a "must-know" topic for you and your organization this year, and we want to bring this information to as many of you as we can reach.

Now more than ever, organizations must understand and address the (insert industry name here) risks, their resources, and their employees. The (insert analyst firm name) Group invites you to join us as we examine these (insert industry name here) challenges and debate the solutions for (insert industry name here) the (insert small, midsize, or enterprise) business. These issues will be positioned against a real-world backdrop of today's overriding (insert industry name here) concerns, including how to reduce complexity, improve control, save money, and open new doors of opportunity.

(Insert strategic partner) Executive Summit
(Insert strategic partner) Partner Solution Center, (insert city and state)

(Insert company name) is announcing and exhibiting the (insert product name) in conjunction with the (insert strategic partner) Executive Summit. (Insert company name here) secured Microsoft's endorsement of the (insert product name) in a supporting statement in the (insert product name) news release.

Event Description: (insert strategic partner) will demonstrate to the worldwide (insert industry) community that it has the best vision, products, solutions, services, and partners to help providers optimize their assets, reduce costs, and deliver profitable new services, and to achieve mutual market success. At this year's summit, (insert strategic partner) will highlight its (insert strategy name) strategy. (Insert strategic partner's CEO) will deliver the keynote address.

TRADE SHOW/EVENTS

(Insert company name) is introducing the (insert product name) at (insert trade show name here). (Insert company name here) is exhibiting in a __'x__" booth at (insert trade show name here), hosting an off-site reception suite, and entering the latest release of (insert company name here) (insert product name here) and the (insert product name) in the Best of Show awards, participating in the trade show closed-circuit television broadcast, and leveraging other trade show opportunities.

Event Description: (insert trade show here) is the world's definitive resource and community for _____, _____ and _____. Companies of all sizes, in all segments of both _____ and _____, leverage (insert trade show event name here) as a leading marketing platform to connect with leading buyers, engage media and analysts, and achieve top visibility and industry profile.

XIV. Public Relations

A successful PR program is a key element for the positioning and public perception of the (insert product name). While marketing, product management and engineering have to work together in order to successfully build the brand, public relations is critical for developing and delivering the right message to the right audience at the right time.

Editorial Perspective on (insert industry here)

While the publications that address the (insert industry here) cover both _____ management and _____ topics, different editors and analysts focus specifically on (insert industry A) and (insert industry B), and a handful of publications are focused specifically on _____. (Insert industry A) is of keen interest, especially in this era.

A recent survey of _____ companies by the (insert market experts) Market Experts Group found that a whopping __ percent expect to increase spending on _____ products right away. Among the big priorities: _____, and beefed-up _____ to create _____ environments for _____.

According to a recent (insert magazine name here) article, "It's no wonder that of the ___ business-technology executives interviewed by (insert magazine name here) in (insert month here), more than half say their companies will increase (insert industry here) spending this year, while __ percent will spend about the same as in 20_ _. Only _percent of managers say their companies have decided to trim (insert industry here) outlays."

Companies of all sizes are concerned about (insert industry here). In all, __ percent of small and large companies say they'll boost their (insert industry here) budgets in 20_); __ percent of midsize businesses will do likewise.

The (insert product name) PR launch is effectively leveraging the media's growing interest in (insert industry here).

PR STRATEGY

Every tool available for communicating to the (insert either small business or midsize or enterprise business) end-user and their business managers must be used to build and enhance the (insert product name) product brand. All press releases highlight competitive advantages. (Insert company name)' Business Development, Engineering, Marketing, and Product Management team will be counted on to help identify and define (insert product name)'s superior and unique features of (insert product name).

Consistent and repeated messages in all communications are emphasizing why (insert product name) is better than other products on the market, are helping to gain market share, are winning consumer confidence, and are establishing a trusted and well-known brand with customers not yet familiar with third-generation (insert industry here). (Insert company here)'s presence at trade shows like (insert trade show event name here) is important and serves as a platform for the key messages. These appearances also give (insert company here) an opportunity to present company products and a road map for the future to media and analysts.

PR will also pitch award and product review opportunities. A targeted approach to top-tier media will help to raise awareness of (insert product name) and receive favorable reviews. Product collateral and press releases, analyst endorsements, and customer success stories will help highlight key competitive advantages.

Analysts as well as media will be briefed on (insert company name here)'s new directions. Media and analyst outreach will communicate (insert company name here)'s overall strategy for the enterprise-class industry. Existing relationships with key media and analysts will be leveraged. Key (insert product name)-related messages will reinforce (insert company name here)'s vision of integration, flexibility, and simplicity. New and creative ways to reach out to an audience will be constantly explored and (insert company name here)'s PR agency will help attract necessary attention to the new product.

(Insert company name here)'s global corporate launch of (insert product name) must be carefully coordinated. Key messages must be consistent and (insert company name here) PR needs to ensure that the company is speaking with the same voice and tone.

An exciting new product, a growing market for third-generation (insert industry here) products, and the (insert company name here) team's focus on the success of the launch will provide the needed fuel to launch the (insert product name) product.

PR OBJECTIVES

- Increase market awareness of (insert company name)
- Effectively highlight the superior quality, security and ease-of-use of (insert product name)
- Differentiate third-generation (insert industry here) and clearly distinguish (insert product name) from (insert competitors' products here) and other third-generation products and services
- Intensively educate the (insert industry) media
- Coordinate global (insert product name) PR launch

(Insert Product Name) PR Calendar

Q1 (Jan.-March)	Q2 (April-June)	Q3 (July-August)	Q4 (Sept.-Dec.)
Event: (Insert Analyst Firm here) Seminars	Alliance Executive Summit	**(Insert Trade show Event here)**	
PR Efforts:	Media/Analyst Tour		
	Product Announcement		
	Alliance Relationship		
		(Insert Trade show Event here) Briefings and Event	
		Product Review(s)	
			Customer Acceptance
			Ongoing Pitching

Q1 (Jan.-March)	Q2 (April-June)	Q3 (July-August)	Q4 (Sept.-Dec.)
Press Releases:	(Insert Analyst Firm here) Seminar Participation		
	(Insert Product Name)		
	Relationship		
		Industry Certification	
		Industry Seminar (Webinar)	
			OEM Relationship
			Customer Acceptance

Q1 (Jan.-March)	Q2 (April-June)	Q3 (July-August)	Q4 (Sept.-Dec.)
Ongoing PR:	**Proactive/ Reactive Media Pitching**		
Media & Analyst Relations			
Product Review Program			
	Speaking Opportunities		
	Global PR Coordination		
		Award Program	
		Third Party Releases	
			Sponsorship / Event Participation
			Web Site Updates
			Coverage Tracking
Internal Communications / Reporting			
PR & Company Collateral			

PRESS RELEASES

Although the product announcement will be the key driver for the (insert product name) launch, it is crucial to also draw media and analyst attention to (insert product name) milestones, such as security certification, customer acceptance, partner alliances, awards, and events.

The (insert product name) product press release will be aggressively pitched to trade publications in order to generate product coverage and review opportunities. The product launch press release will highlight key benefits and competitive advantage of (insert product name) and include as available analyst endorsement and beta customer reference statements. Ongoing newsworthy milestones will be vital to the success of the product launch. Goals of the press release program include:

- Create and implement a series of milestones that provide the basis for the press release calendar
- Communicate key messages in every press release
- Highlight (insert product name)'s competitive advantages
- Highlight all unique and superior product features and outline how (insert product name) is different from (insert competitors product names here) and superior to third-generation secure access alternatives from the competition
- Targeted media and analyst outreach for each press release
- Leverage announcements for different pitch angles

PRESS MATERIAL

The (insert product name) press kit contains the following information pieces: company profile sheet, product milestones, market driver's sheet, product data sheet, and white paper(s). The material is available from the press area of the (insert company name here) positioning and advantages, and provides the content basis for an online demo. Goals for press materials include:

- Develop (insert product name) press-specific documents
- Continue to develop press collateral
- Update developed press kit material and continuously create/ update online press kit
- Develop creative (insert product name)-related press material

AWARDS AND REVIEW PROGRAM

The awards program is vitally important to validate (insert product name). Since the (insert industry here) market in the United States is the world's most competitive, it is crucial to dedicate resources to evaluation units and supporting the evaluation process. Relationships with key media contacts are being leveraged. Goals of the awards and review program include:

- Focus on product awards from top-tier publications
- Aggressively pitch (insert product name) to review editors and test labs
- Editorial Calendar pitching and press release outreach serve as indirect support
- Proactively pitch nonproduct awards (top prestigious awards)— *Red Herring* (Top 50 private companies), *Fortune* (Fortune 100), *Computerworld* (Emerging Companies), etc.
- Leverage favorable reviews and awards

MEDIA RELATIONS

Generating exposure through proactive relations with target trade press is the first step in media relations to introduce (insert product name). Business press will be pitched regarding the trend toward (insert new product update), and reinforced with customer acceptance. Goals of the media relations program include:

- Develop and maintain targeted media list
- Extend and develop relationships with influential media contacts
- Maintain proactive media outreach
- Creative media outreach (out-of-the-box thinking—security shootout)
- Maintain ongoing editorial calendar pitching
- Pitch CEO profile and company story
- Pitch press releases
- Arrange media briefings on an ongoing basis
- Educate media on benefits of a third-generation approach
- Provide broad range of collateral for different levels of media interests
- Maintain comprehensive media list
- Focus on a broad range of media (print, online, and broadcast)

INDUSTRY ANALYST PROGRAM

Analysts of leading analyst firms need to be briefed about (insert product name) and updated on a regular basis, since analysts serve as trusted third parties for media contacts. Goals of the industry analyst program include:

- Maintain and update analyst list
- Keep analysts updated and in the loop on recent product and partnership announcements
- Conduct analyst briefings (in person / phone) on a regular basis
- Leverage and use analyst knowledge for quotes in press releases, media pitches, etc.
- Focus on key analyst firms, including larger and smaller firms

MEDIA AND ANALYST INTRODUCTORY TOUR

The (insert product name) is being introduced by (insert your CEO/ president name here) through a Media and Analyst Tour in the United States and Europe, consisting of telephone and in-person briefings supported by a PowerPoint presentation. Tour goals are:

- (Insert industry here) reference
- (Insert industry here) coverage in key publications
- (Insert industry here) product review opportunities

VIEWPOINT OPPORTUNITIES

(Insert company name here) white papers and other viewpoints will provide the basis for submission abstracts for speaking opportunities at industry conferences and bylined articles in industry publications. Goals of the viewpoints program include:

- Target relevant conferences and bylined article opportunities
- Develop and submit presentation and article abstracts
- Distribute press release regarding speaking opportunity if applicable

EVENTS AND SPONSORSHIPS

The (insert product name) is being previewed at the (insert analysts name here) the (insert industry here) seminar, announced at the (insert alliance) Executive Summit, and introduced at the (insert trade show event name here) trade show in (insert city, state location here). If budget allows, a launch event will introduce (insert product name) to (insert trade show name here) attendees including press and analysts. Follow-on events such as a Webinar and exhibiting at other trade show will provide additional (insert product name) introduction opportunities that can be of interest to the media. Goals of the event program include:

- Introduce (insert product name) at (insert trade show name here)
- Schedule media and analyst briefings for each event
- Develop and implement creative ideas to reach new media at trade shows
- Depending on budget, (insert company name) will exhibit at and/or sponsor additional events

GLOBAL PR

All activities initiated by (insert company name) corporate marketing will be coordinated for global execution by (insert company name) corporate and regional PR agencies, and as possible through distributors' PR efforts. Goals of global PR include:

- Coordinate and support global PR efforts (international trade shows, etc.)
- Distribute press releases internally and provide support for translation, etc.
- Ensure consistent global messaging
- Delegate and manage international interview requests
- Develop global media database

PRESS/ANALYST TARGETS

(Please use the follow list of names as a starting point. If you contact a specific publication and the person mentioned is no longer there, simply ask for their replacement.)

Washington DC

Information Week	Stephanie Stahl	DC
CRN	Sara Driscoll, Editor	UK
USA Today	Dan Vergano , Kevin Maney	Arlington, VA
Washington Post	Dan Beyers and Ariana Eunjung Cha	DC

Boston

Aberdeen	John Pearson	Boston
AMR/Gartner	Joseph Baylock	Boston
IDC	Jason Smolek,	Framingham
Giga/Forrester	Stan Schatt, Thomas Mendel	Cambridge
Hurwitz	Rich Ptak	Cambridge
Forrester	Galen Schreck	Cambridge
Network World	Tim Greene, Neal Weinberg, Keith Shaw	Southborough
Network Computing	Mike Fratto, Editor	Waltham
Everything Channel	Jennifer Hagendorf Follett	Waltham
eWeek	Dennis Fisher	Medford
Computerworld	James Cope	Framingham
Fast Company	Dan Nosowitz	Boston
Forbes	Daniel Lyons (networking)	Cambridge
Inc. Technology	Jill Maxwell	Boston

New York

Information Week	Andrew Cory-Murray	Manhasset
ZDNet	Ryan Naraine	Long Island
Network Computing	Mike Fratto (security)	Upstate NYPC Magazine
AP	Nick Jesdanun,	NYC

Bloomberg BusinessWeek	Jim Zemlin, Dan Heintzelman	NYC
BusinessWeek.com	Staccey Higginbtham	NY
Forbes	Neil Weinberg	
Fortune	Rick Kirkland, Jennifer Reingold	NYC
NY Times	Randal Archibold, Damon Darlin	NYC
Red Herring	Alex Vieux, Joel Dreyfuss	NYC
Smart Business	Don Steinberg	NYC
Research Board	Brendan Conway	NYC

APPENDIX A

MEDIA AND ANALYST LIST, EDITORIAL OPPORTUNITIES

(Please use the follow list of names as a starting point. If you contact a specific publication and the person mentioned is no longer there, simply ask for their replacement.)

SELECT MEDIA, ANALYSTS AND INFLUENCERS FOCUSING ON TECHNOLOGY MARKET

eWeek:	Dennis Fisher, Cameron Sturdevant
ComputerWorld:	James Cope, Dan Verton
Everything Channel:	Larry Hooper, Marcia Savage
IDG News Service:	Sam Costello
InfoWorld:	Phil Krill
Information Security:	Robert Westervelt
Information Week:	George Hulme
Technology Writer:	Leon Erlanger
SC InfoSecNews:	Steve Gold
Network World:	Tim Greene
Network Magazine:	Doug Allen
Network Computing:	Mike Fratto

PC Magazine:	Matt Sarrell
SC Magazine:	Illena Armstrong
Security Magazine:	Bill Zalud
UBM TechWeb.com:	David Berlind

INDUSTRY ANALYSTS

Zeus Kerravala	Yankee Group
Erin Traudt	IDC
Jason Smolek	IDC
John Andrews	Giga Information Group.
Fern Halper	Hurwitz Group
Ian Williams	RSA Security
Alan Zeichick	Camden Associates
Sterling Auty	J.P.Morgan

COVERAGE OF TECHNOLOGY BASELINE

(Please use the follow list of names as a starting point. If you contact a specific publication and the person mentioned is no longer there, simply ask for their replacement.)

Business 2.0	Dylan Tweeney
Business Week	Steve Hamm, Alex Salkever & Jim Kerstetter
CIO	Sarah Scalet, Tom Kaneshige
CNET	Gwendolyn Mariano, Sergio Non, Ben Charny, Robert Lemos
Computerworld	Dan Verton, James Cope, Frank Hayes
CRN	Marcia Savage, Larry Hooper
eWeek	Max Smetannikov, Dennis Fisher, Timothy Dyck, Jim Rapoza, Cameron Sturdevant
Forbes	Eric Pfeiffer
Fortune	David Kirkpatrick
Information Security	Christopher King and Curtis Dalton
Information Week	George Hulme
Infosecnews.com	Steve Gold (Information Security News)

InfoWorld	Stephen Lee, Sam Costello, Tom Yager
Internet.com	Clint Boulton
Internet Telephony	Robert Bova
Internet World	Sarah L. Roberts-Witt, Keeno Ahmed, Leon Erlanger
Net Economy	Christine Zimmerman
Network Computing	Mike Fratto
Network Magazine	Doug Allen
Network World	Tim Greene, Toni Kistner, Joel Snyder, Deni Connor
PC Magazine	Jim Seymour (Seymour Group) Karen Bannen
PC World	Sam Costello, Brad Grimes
Red Herring	Alan Zeichick
SC Magazine	Bob Walder
Security Magazine	Bill Zalud
Smart Business	Steve Mollman
TechWeb.com	Scot Finnie
The451.com	Ian Jacobs
VAR Business	Chandra Steele, Lloyd Tanaka, Rich Cirillo
ZDNet	Jerald Murphy, Michael Deignan, Michael Coursey

Appendix B

Market Requirements Document; MRD Outline

Hardware

The _____ should use the _____ chassis, motherboard, CPU, network interfaces, hard disk, and _____ accelerator as the _____ series.

The front bezel should have the appearance of (insert targeted appearance/style) <u>(insert industry here)</u> product. The industrial design should communicate _____.

The front panel must have a two-line LCD display with a minimum of forty columns. The front panel should at the very least show the product name and system load. Any more advanced displays should be controllable by the <u>(insert customer type here)</u>. (i.e. the end user should be able to choose what he does and does not want displayed).

Product Premise

_____ based on _____ technology present a challenge to _____ due to the complexity of the client and server side software, the client rollout, and end-user training.

We assert that a significant amount of the _____ users only require a small (and simple) subset of _____ protocols in order to accomplish their work. Thus, it should be possible to deploy a _____ based on the _____ protocol that leverages the software already installed on the typical _____ system.

By using already installed applications _____, end users are no longer required to roll out _____ and _____ thereby saving in both the installation and in support.

For additional information on the product premise, please see the _____ Business Plan.

PRODUCT CONCEPT

The _____ is a device that resides between the _____ and _____. Using _____ enhanced software, customers connect to this device where the incoming commands are _____ using the (insert your product here), and then forwarded to the appropriate next component. For version 1.0, we will support the following protocols: _____, _____, _____, and _____.

The "home page" on the device will list all of the available internal settings. The user can then click their application of choice. Communication to/from the user will be relayed through this interface.

The (insert product here) will only have a minimal command line interface necessary for setting the management. The rest of the configuration should be handled via the User Interface/WebUI.

FEATURES

FEATURE A

The user should be able to have their users .... We must document any schema requirements for the ...

FEATURE B

The user should be able to have their users ...

Note: Feature B may not be able to ... If this is the case, be sure to document the limitations.

FEATURE C

The user should be able to have their ...

Note: Feature C may not be able to ... If this is the case, be sure to document the limitations.

FEATURE D

The user should be able to configure ... Thought of as a simple series of tables; the effect should be as follows:

USER LIST

- User ID [key]
- Login
- MDR1 Password

GROUP LIST

- Group ID [key]
- Group Name

URL LIST

- URL ID [key]
- Host
- URL

If the user is allowed _____. *Note that the method and planned relationships are verified is left up to engineering.* The above schema is for demonstration purposes only.

FEATURE E

The _____ component of this feature should inherit all of the features from the company's OS code base. At a minimum, this should include the following features:

X: ABC (1024 bits)
Y: DEF (168 bits)
Z: GHI (128 bits)

The user should be able to configure some ... for fast performance, high speed, very-high speed performance.

PROTOCOL- _____

The user should connect to the ... For the first connection from the user, this should redirect them to a Web page where they may login.

The Web page should appear attractive to the user and optionally have a user specified image on it (e.g. a company logo, etc.). The page should be branded to the customer, not to the company.

The user will be able to click on a site that they wish to go to.

ADMIN-WEBUI-BASE

The administrators' user interface should be very easy to use and follow the same theme as specified by the company UI project.

The WebUI should work across the following browsers:

Internet Explorer	Microsoft Corporation
Firefox	Mozilla Corporation
Chrome	Google
Safari	Apple Inc.
Opera	Opera Software ASA
Netscape	Navigator Netscape Communications Corporation (now part of AOL)
SeaMonkey	Mozilla Foundation
K-Meleon	kmeleonbrowser.org
Amaya	W3C
Maxthon Browser	Maxthon
Flock	Flock, Inc.
Midori	TwoToasts.de
Slim Browser	FlashPeak
KidRocket	KidRocket.org

The WebUI should be *very* easy to use and be *very* consistent. The top-level page should offer access to online help, documentation in PDF, Wizards, and direct links to the advanced configuration screen.

All documentation in PDF form should ship with the product. Product upgrades should include updates to the documentation as well. Online help should be written in clear, concise, and proper English.

The technical setup interface should show the status of the overall system. The user should be able to monitor one of the following graphs, updates every sixty seconds: number of users, bandwidth, or load. From the technical setup interface the user should be able to go to the configuration screens and the top-level page.

ADMIN-WEBUI-WIZARDS

The WebUI should offer a series of wizards for common configurations. The wizards should not require more than four to five steps, with each step asking for only a small amount of related information. Where defaults can be selected, defaults should be available. An administrator new to the product should be able to set up and create a basic configuration (login/password, access anything on the inside) using wizards alone.

WEB-BASED MARKETING

One of the most visible components of your marketing efforts is Web-based marketing. As a relatively new—and fast evolving—medium, the Web is often misunderstood. Trends destined for a short shelf life are hailed as the business model for the next generation, prompting CEOs and board members to throw many millions of dollars at poorly thought-out ideas just to be "first to market."

The belief that putting up an e-commerce Web site will automatically bring in tens of millions of new revenue dollars is a fallacy. Search engine optimization (SEO) is a falsehood of fast, easy money. The Web is actually a new business unit or distribution unit for your company and, as such, needs to be carefully thought out and developed with long-term profitability in mind.

Your company will want a new and improved Web site up and generating income almost overnight. While that is impossible, this chapter will kick-start your process and help reduce your time to market.

How to use this chapter's materials: "The Catching Customers in Your Web" essay will provide you with insight for developing your e-commerce strategy, while "New Media Strategies" will break down many of the new marketing mediums developing alongside e-commerce. The to-do lists and templates will help you organize your thoughts, get the feedback you need from around the company, and filter out much of the time wasted when approaching Web-based marketing from a blank slate.

Included in this chapter:
- Catching Customers in Your Web
- New Media Strategies
- To-Do:
- Planning a Website
- Launch a New Product on Your Website
- Products Tasks
- Viral Strategies
- Templates
- Website Kickoff Meeting Agenda
- Website Specifications for a Bid
- Proposal for Building a Web site
- Web site Outline Approval Form

CATCHING CUSTOMERS IN YOUR WEB

If you have ever wandered the aisles of the furniture store IKEA, you know the feeling of a bricks-and-mortar environment that is focused on the customer. Instead of the conventional furniture store with row after row of sofas, loveseats, and tables, IKEA's wares are displayed in compelling, homelike settings that portray the lifestyle you would enjoy through a living room or kitchen filled with coordinated accessories. IKEA is designed that way because savvy retailers understand the value of "pavilions," each focused on an area of the home with instant gratification and immediate sales in mind. Your business Web site should be designed with similar values.

What many retailers don't understand is that the consumer can sense arrogance or indifference wafting out of a store in less than three seconds. Shoppers need to feel cared for in every venue. The store's mission must be aligned with the customer's needs and values. You don't walk in and find yourself staring at a floor filled with sofas. It is important to understand that your company's Web site is a virtual equivalent to a retail store, with the same upside for conveying value within the visitor's brief initial threshold of interest and the same penalties for portraying your products and solutions as a "floor filled with sofas."

It's also key to understand the power of your brand and the increasing importance of e-business, twin pillars of the successful Web presence. Be wary of using your Web site to portray an undifferentiated collection of technology. Don't forget the "Why do they need it? Why do they want it?" part of the equation.

FIRST IMPRESSIONS COUNT

Just as in a retail store, the Web site starts with the first impression. Like the retail store environment, the Web site should utilize its entire "space." The worst thing you can do is to prevent people from getting beyond the entrance to the store. The Web equivalent is a home page that requires the visitor to view a time-consuming Flash animation before entering the site. One, two, three seconds, and, unless you're lucky, the visitor is gone, vanished into cyberspace, probably searching Google for a link to your competitor's Web site. The more effective alternative is to display animated or graphical elements in a restricted area of the home page, with other informational elements calling for attention while the graphics play a more subliminal role.

Often, the most important customers don't actually purchase anything from your company. They're the ones who strongly influence others, and the ones that help tell your story. These include consultants and investors, press and analysts, friends and family—anyone who visits your Web site should be able to understand your company's vision and what your products promise just by looking at the home page.

Successful companies do a good job of leading visitors to their Web site through effective use of search engines, such as Google and Yahoo! Your meta tag descriptions, text portrayed in standard html (not embedded in image maps), and the related links associated with your site enable search engines' Web crawlers to "understand" your site, which translates into better placement on keyword searches. Your own site should enable keyword searches, and, if your products are complex, consider implementing a parametric search engine to enable multicriteria searches by capacities, component types, and other specifications.

STREAMLINING THE CUSTOMER EXPERIENCE

Companies with the best Web presence typically also do the best job of tracking what customers do on their sites in order to continuously simplify and streamline the visitor's experience. Logs of paths that customers take and where they left off enable you to make it easy for customers to navigate your site and find what they want with as few clicks as possible. Customers may need several different ways to locate products and information. No more than three clicks should take the visitor to any area of the site.

Web performance testing tools enable you to understand how your site will work under peak load conditions with varying combinations of hardware, Web servers, databases, and networks. Web performance testing services such as Keynote evaluate your site's performance in real-world situations from various locations. Its one thing to click through your Web site on a high-bandwidth local network, possibly quite another if you're one of a thousand concurrent users, connected via a dial-up modem from Toledo or Timbuktu. Web traffic management and optimization technologies can accelerate your Web infrastructure.

Content delivery networks can speed content delivery. There's simply no excuse for a slow Web site.

DEALING WITH REAL-TIME INFORMATION

Most companies have "interesting" Web sites; great companies have "interested" Web sites that thrive on customer feedback. Handling customers' e-mails is vital. If the customer or prospect takes the time to send you an e-mail inquiry, it's equivalent to having them sit in the recliner in the retail showroom. How you respond either holds their interest or signals that you're not that interested in their business. Once you log their inquiry in your database, consider routing it beyond the technical support group to product managers, marketing managers, or engineering teams to get your entire company involved with the customer.

With real-time information flowing into your Web site, organizing this data by product or solution provides a window into your Web presence that can help your entire company understand what products are in demand, what information helps the sale, and what problems are being encountered. Customer support inquiries should be responded to within hours, not days, and monitored by top management. And invaluable customer information should be collected to answer questions, such as: How many visitors were registered users? Of the registered users, what information did they read, which products did they evaluate or buy, and why did they consider them? Based on their survey answers or buying habits, are their interests and buying habits aligned with the way the content on your site is organized? Even though you may not have implemented a complete business intelligence system, you can start capturing vital cookie information and other Web site traffic data now and connect to analysis systems later.

KNOWING THE CUSTOMER

Visitors should be required to register to receive white papers or other in-depth information. Partners should be empowered with private areas of the site that provide pricing, competitive information, sales guides, recommended configurations, support FAQs, and other sales support information. Trusted partners should be able to log sales, confirm capacity and pricing, and place orders, which help you plan production and gain visibility into the end customers' accounts. End users with established purchasing track records could be empowered with pricing and availability information for small-quantity, quick turnaround orders.

Customer should be able to maintain and update their profiles, which in turn should be linked to customer relationship management systems. If the customer moves from San Jose to Sacramento and takes the time to update his profile, your sales force should be equipped with this information without having to chase down the customer. For the best relationships with top customers, consider equipping your sales reps with the templates to build a personalized Web site for key accounts. Combine that with systematic e-mails that inform customers of new product releases, critical support information, product discounts, and other information. You get the idea—make sure the customer knows how much you care about their business.

Security creates a feeling of trust. Today, the use of encrypted Secure Sockets Layer (SSL) connections is extending beyond the protection of e-commerce transactions to every aspect of Web content. It's worth considering encrypting every connection to your site that requires two-way interaction with the customer. The worst thing that can happen is for a hacker to know more about your customer than you do.

Your Web presence says more about your company and its intended relationships with its partners and customers than any advertisement or glossy brochure could ever communicate. Those companies that "get it" are those with a strong point of view, who convey to the customer a sense of trust and concern. On the other end of the continuum are those companies whose Web sites portray their products as the proverbial "floor full of sofas." It's readily possible to use your Web site to bring your partners and customer much more closely into your inner circle of trust. Your Web presence communicates an attitude of caring. Or it's one, two, three seconds, they're gone.

# # # #

Yesterday's Marketing Model on a Consumer Relationship Management Individual Level Touch-Points

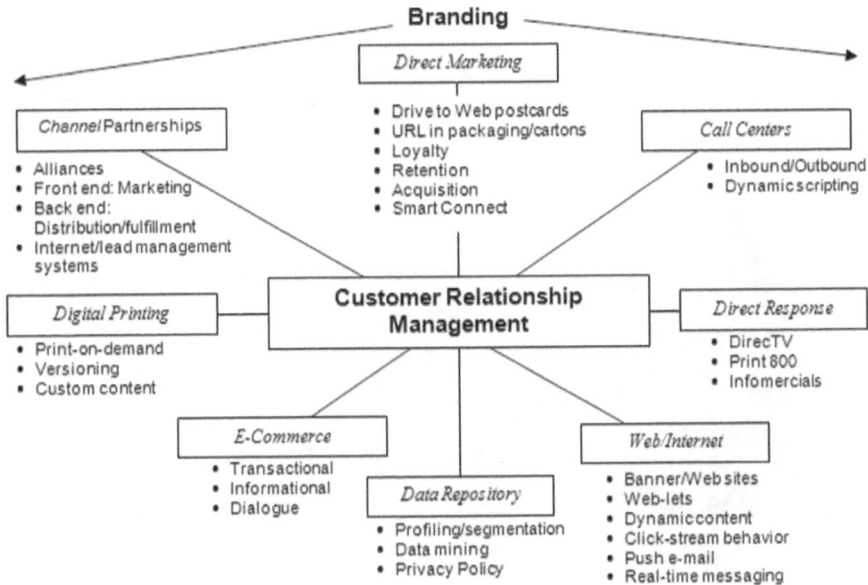

Today's D2C Business Model with the New "Digital Plan" Overlay

To reach the consumer masses there is a need for a "digital plan." The days of the one screen only strategy are over. In addition to delivering products and services across traditional marketing communication methods, there is a need to add new broadband channels, over cell phones/handheld devices, via video games, interactive media (where things click), and more.

Web/Simulcasts/Broadband/Interactive/Podcasts

Cellular/Wireless/Hand Held Devices

Direct/email Campaigns

Public Relations

Channel Promotions

Television/Radio/XM Radio

Print

Destination Marketing

Question: Why does your Web site deserve to be #1?
- Because I have the lowest prices
- Because I have better customer service
- Because I've been in business longer
- Because no one does this better than me
- None of the above

The correct answer is:
None of the above

Actually, all of those things can be a factor as to why a Web site might appear higher up in the search results, but none of them represent the real reason. What is that real reason why any site deserves to be #1? That can be summed up as this: It provides something unique, interesting, compelling, or valuable that my visitors cannot find anywhere else.

Destination marketing can be defined as: The act of developing a Web site to become a desired destination for people looking for the product, services, or information that you provide. In other words, destination marketing is SEO and SEM without compromising rankings for conversions or conversions for rankings.

A goal for your Web site is to be a user friendly, information-rich, unique destination that establishes trust and leaves a positive impression in the minds of your visitors.

The art/science of SEO should ultimately be about developing and implementing a solid destination marketing campaign that gives people a reason to want to visit and/or buy from you. If you want to stand out in a sea of thousands of other Web sites, you simply have no other choice.

There are many kinds of marketing strategies that can be effective in the short term, but destination marketing is easily the most effective and long lasting. You can drive traffic to your site via commercials, link bait, ads, or top rankings, but traffic, by itself, doesn't create customers. Yes, an increase in conversions usually does correspond with an increase in traffic, but are these one-time buyers or long-term customers? All of these things can contribute to improvement in sales and conversions, but nothing builds a business like building a repeat customer base.

Not only that, but each customer will undoubtedly refer many people to you over the course of the years, another great benefit of creating a destination Web site. A satisfied customer can produce a dozen more, but a customer that returns to your Web site time and time again because you have created a "destination" produces hundreds more.

Seven building blocks of a destination Web site:

1. Expert information
2. Usability
3. Web site design
4. Unique selling proposition (USP)
5. Time and presence
6. Voice
7. Trust and credibility

BECOMING A DESTINATION WEB SITE:

With thousands of Web sites competing for a top ten spot in the search results, only those sites that have set themselves apart from the rest as the best destination for that query will achieve first page status. That's what destination marketing is all about: not achieving, but truly deserving a top ranking on the search engines.

SOCIAL MARKETING

Bring a strong sense of the digital community to (insert company name here). Focus on creating, facilitating, and participating effectively in key conversations about the (insert company name here) brands on blogs and other online social media channels. Take these steps to effectively build and leverage digital media for scale, reach, and community building across online communities, virtual worlds, and social networks:

- Monitor relevant social media for important trends related to specific brands and entertainment properties.
- Create and maintain visible MySpace, FaceBook, Twitter, Loopt, Friendster, FlickR, Digg, Fark accounts and other social media profiles.
- Create and maintain visible Linked-In, Plaxo, YouTube, TokBox accounts for professionals and other social media profiles.
- Report on the effectiveness of social site placement.
- Generate buzz and interest in various forms of digital media such as online videos, blog posts, news articles, images, and more.
- Maintain a daily social outreach online for the (insert company name here) brands and sales ventures.

(Insert CEO/president name here) personal brand building via social marketing:
- (Insert CEO/president name here)'s personal life is part of their professional brand. Casually on: MySpace, LinkedIn, Plaxo, FaceBook, and even YouTube. The opportunity is to help them properly network and raise positive impressions when industry

members and fellow (insert company name here) colleagues Google their names.

- Focus on social status online and immediately post professional images and short videos.

- Proactively solicit industry people to write references and referrals and place them online.

- Post any volunteering efforts or leadership roles.

- Develop and deliver three speeches, videotape them, and post them on YouTube and on (insert CEO/president name here)'s online Web portfolio.

- Start (insert CEO/president name here) blogs.

- Have (insert CEO/president name here) write book reviews on Amazon and Barnes & Noble online.

- Have (insert CEO/president name here) author four articles and publish them in a magazine or blog.

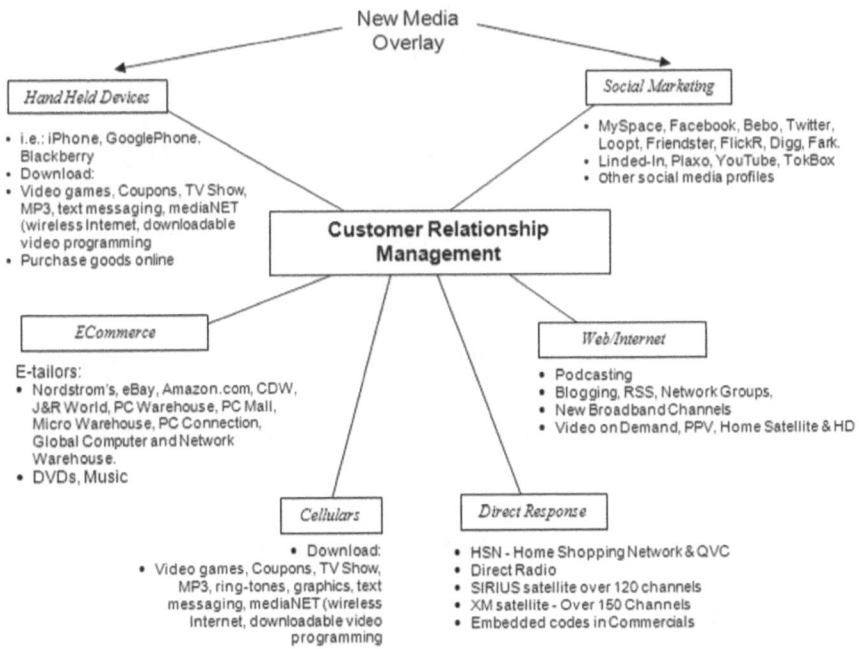

CUSTOMER DEMOGRAPHICS

Having direct to consumer media business expertise is necessary to effectively leverage your customer's demographics. Reaching consumers in today's marketplace requires approaches and tools that extend far beyond textbook marketing strategies.

It is imperative you understand your consumer segmentation and conduct target audiences benchmarking. Is your customer middle class, blue collar, mass market, family brand? Do you have a foothold with "Family First," which is comprised of higher income that benefits from larger disposable income collect easier premium pricing?

All companies need to create a "Message Guide" for customers and consumers by understanding their wants and needs and applying its innovation to products that enhance the quality of life or work. Your messaging has to have a strategic set of objectives to increase awareness of your brand and key brand attributes among target audiences to generate consumer interest, excitement, and word-of-mouth for your brand and products.

CUSTOMER SEGMENTATION PRIORITIES

Know who your consumers are—specifically. Know if they are evenly divided between males and females. Do they range in age from as young as 13 to as golden as 65? Do their educations, incomes, and lifestyles vary? How do they spend their leisure time and their leisure-time money?

Below are five neat consumer categories, which help target and focus organization in efficient and effective ways.

Dream Seekers are young and energetic, just starting out in life, and they use technology to make things better for themselves and their families.

Family Firsts are generally older and more concerned with making sure they have the latest technologies so that their children and other family members can benefit. These consumers have already decided that technology is probably not for them, but it is important for those they care about.

Tech Status are the peacocks of life. They like to see and be seen with the latest and greatest technology.

Tech Enabled consumers use technology to get their work done or get ahead. They're passionate, driven people, with high income and education.

Amuse Me consumers are kids that like to have fun with technology products or are older or retired people who spend a good deal of time enjoying the entertainment or enhancement values of various technology products.

Consumer Categories Summary

Dream Seeker	to make things better for self and family
Family First	to advance the next generation (of family)
Tech Status	as a badge of belonging to contemporary life
Tech-Enabled	to support drive for efficiency, productivity, and advancement
Amuse Me	to enable drive for affordable pleasure and escape

People are listening to music on their phones, some are watching videos, some are deep in multiplayer games; a few are even talking. There's this massive group of young, tech-savvy consumers as for example searching for their favorite sport idol. They not only want video games, ring tones, blog entries, screensavers they just may buy all products.

Your brand should be a lifestyle depiction of what the brand is supposed to mean. Digital content should be the embodiment of the (insert company name here) brand. At the center of the brand is the whole notion of a connected community, which is represented by an artifact that happens to be a PC or handheld device such as a phone. But it's not the artifact that matters—"it's the (insert company name here) lifestyle."

- Planning a Web Site
- Launch a New Product on Your Website
- Products Tasks
- Viral Strategies

Planning a Web Site

- Online marketing will only work if your company understands marketing
- Online marketing means a lot more than having a Web site
- Online marketing is only a small percent of all marketing

The insight is to continue marketing with traditional media. Your Web site needs marketing.

The options are many:

- Multiple links to other sites
- Banners leading to our site
- Search engines directing browsers to our site
- Chat conferences heralding our site
- Recommendations of our site by Internet powers
- E-mailing to parties demonstrably interested in learning about the topics covered on our site
- Mentioning your site in our e-mail signature
- Versions of your press kit to publish our site online
- Connecting with as many other online entities as possible

All can contribute to making your site part of the online community, an Internet landmark to our prospects, a not-to-be-missed feature of the Web.

Promote the site on:

- Corporate, product, and classified ads
- Stationery
- Business cards
- Signs
- Brochures and other collateral
- Packages
- Business forms
- Gift certificates
- Reprints of PR articles
- Radio

- Direct marketing campaigns

Promotions will lure them to your site; killer content will cause them to make return trips. Pay extra close attention to how easy it is to find your company. Does your site appear near the top in all the search engines? Is it on the first page of any classified search? Can visitors directly access the data they need rather than having to navigate through many unnecessary pages?

Prospects really want: safety, convenience, speed, service, information, personal attention, and good values.

- What is the immediate, short-term goal of your Web site?
- What specific action do we want visitors to take?
- What are your specific objectives for the long term?
- Who do you want to visit your site?
- What solutions or benefits can you offer to these visitors?
- What data should your site provide to achieve your primary goal?
- What information can you provide to encourage them to act right now?
- What questions do you get asked the most on the telephone?
- What questions and comments do you hear most at trade shows?
- What data should your site provide to achieve your secondary goal?
- Where does your target audience look for infractions?
- What may be the reasons you don't sell as much as you'd like to?
- Who is your most astute competitor?
- Does your competitor have a Web site?
- What are ways you can distinguish yourselves from your competitors?
- How important is price to your target audience?

How to Launch a New Product on Your Web Site

[PM] = Project Manager
[AAE] = Assistant Account Executive
[GD] = Graphic Designer
[Prog.] = Programmer

Launch Site

- Collect the product and packaging images (TIF and JPG) from [PM]
- Collect the product docs (data sheet, ad copy, FAQ, comp, retail facts, positioning, q-cards) from [PM]
- Resize images as needed. [GD]
- Post the images and files to the Launch Site (as either "Coming Soon" or "Now Available") [PM, AAE]

Images

- Pull the product and product packaging images from the company product launch site [GD]
- Resize the product and packaging images for the pressroom. Package image to approx 188x120 [GD]
- Create a new channel graphic (if a new product category), and a new header graphic (if a new subcategory) [GD]
- Create a new DHTML nav image (if a new product category) [GD]
- Create a new category image for the products landing page, / products.asp (if a new product category) [GD]
- Create new matrix headers (if the new product has new features not offered with other products in the matrix) [GD or Prog.]
- Create new home page feature graphic for the product [GD]
- Last Step—Upload all channel, header, and product images to the Web server using the site admin tools [GD, PM or AAE]

PDFs

- Pull the product PDFs from the company product launch site [PM or AAE]
- Upload PDF using the site admin tools [PM or AAE]

Product Information Pages

- Upload product information using the admin tool. [PM or AAE]
    - product name/number
    - category
    - subcategory
    - small product image
    - large product image
    - link to support site
    - link to online store (once the product is live on staging Launch Site)
- Upload the key features from the ad copy doc from the Launch Site [PM or AAE]
- Upload and format the data sheet html from the PDF datasheet from the company Launch Site [PM or AAE]

Product Matrix

- Update the product matrix with the appropriate boxes checked … specs from company [Prog.]
- Insert new columns and column header graphics (if the new product has new features not offered with other products in the matrix) [Prog.]

Pressroom

- Upload the product press release info using the admin tools and the press releases provided by company [PM or AAE]

- Update the pressroom image library using the resized TIF from Designer [Prog.]

Home Page

Upload and relink the new featured product graphic [Prog.]

Launching Web-based Products

Write initial blog copy
Provide ongoing blog support
Edit Key Messaging Document (KMD) and support revisions
Edit customer e-mails
Write copy for product combined Web site
Edit/proof Web site revisions
Write/edit copy for fact sheet

Revise current product collateral (fact sheet, product overview, etc.)
Create PR Reviewers' Guide
Write copy for parent corporation Web site
Write/edit copy for banners
Write/edit copy for landing page(s)
Write/edit copy for other direct response DR media (print, direct mail, etc.)
Edit events list
Create product logo
Planning for new product Web site (integrated product and corporate site)
Develop creative concepts in preparation for launch
Start development on new product Web site
Style guide for product Web site (detailed information to guide developer)
Log-In Page
Forgot Password Page
Forgot Password Page E-mail Sent
Reset Password Page
Expired Link Page
Press & Awards Page
Awards Page
Press Releases Page
Press Coverage Page
Events Page
Press Kit Page
Industry Opinions Page
Page Not Found Page

About Us Page
Become a Partner Page
Worldwide Offices Page
Product Case Studies Page
Product White Papers Page

Home Page
Product How It Works
Product How It Works for Your Clients
Product Features
Product Technology
Product Reliability
Product Security
Product Management
Product Integration
Product Overview
Product Unattended Support
Solutions Page
Product Solutions Page

Home Page
Product FAQs
FAQs
Product Comparison Matrix
Product Comparison Guide
Site Map
Sales Contact Form
Sales Contact Thank You Form
Product Support Page
Product Customer Care Contact Form
Product Customer Care Contact Form Thank You Page

Tasks
There are 35+ e-mails due for release divided into three phases.
Phase I - welcome (trailers and buyers), trial expiration, trial auto-conversion, trial cancellation (ac off), and credit card declined
Phase II

Phase III
All template designs and HTML programming due for the base templates:
1. Tab design
2. Postcard design
3. Two-column design

Support and Enhance the Forum and Blog
Produce Landing Page - LP to support beta user recruitment

Minisites for business partner promotion of product

Develop newsroom items, LPs, and e-mails to support product launch
Add product info to Corp and other product sites
Regular updates to product Web site after FEC becomes available

Web Development Tasks

Code online campaigns that support growth of customer-base
Upload new creative assets to various product Web sites
Create live Webinar landing pages and e-mail blasts in database, possibly in several versions/designs to generate the most leads possible
Code newsletters for both existing product customers and prospect customers
Create archived Webinar landing pages in database

VIRAL STRATEGIES

GOALS AND OBJECTIVES

- Drive purchases within CPO parameters
- (Cost Per Order—cost of advertising based on the number of orders received). Also called Cost Per Transaction
- Increase brand awareness
- Increase overall market penetration/share

KEY PERFORMANCE INDICATORS

Generate company Web site visits
Generate referrals
Generate new registrants/leads through promotions (and migration into CRM program)
Convert visitors to customers

PLANNING ASSUMPTIONS

- Brand has a powerful, untapped asset: its evangelists (loyal users)
- These evangelists can create momentum and groundswell at launch
- Viral marketing can seed the market and further ignite brand evangelists
- Layering in aggressive brand/response tactics after viral and evangelist programs have started will best deliver against goals and objectives
- Coming back into the market with a post launch promotion will further drive campaign performance

EVANGELIST PROGRAM

- User evangelist program
  - "Connectors" would be recruited to participate in a formal program to evangelize the product through their social and professional networks

- Potentially, a reward structure would be implemented to prompt participants
- The hub of the program would be a Web site containing:
  - Award program sign-up/tracking
  - Community and feedback features
  - Promotional information re: (product or software version) upgrade
  - Tools to support advocacy

- User evangelist program
  - Awards program (tentative)
  - Provide _____ of (insert company here) _____ at no charge for every new purchase evangelist enlists (up to a year free)
  - For additional purchases, offer gift cards to iTunes or electronic retailers (Best Buy)
  - Offer Beta testing/early upgrades to (product or software version) next year
  - Develop a quarterly newsletter/send e-mails with updates on (insert company name here) and other related news (i.e.: vacations, lifestyle)—as well as sneak peeks at marketing materials
  - New commercials, etc.

Evangelist program (continued)

- A successful long-term program will be driven not only by reward incentives but also by the opportunity to be connected
  - With a product and a company they feel strongly about
  - With a like-minded network
- To that end, the program should provide:
  - Premium access to resources/information
  - Support/dialogue with the company
  - Opportunities to connect
  - Cross-promotions with other relevant products/brands
- Launch a viral campaign among consumers using a mix of online and guerilla tactics

- Outdoor events/street teams
- Microsite
- Viral e-mail
- Engage consumers in an entertaining, unexpected way to build awareness and to encourage them to "pay it forward" to friends and colleagues
  - Building awareness
  - Driving interest
  - Creating demand
- Evangelist recruitment
  - Analyze and segment existing database
- Geography
- Purchasing patterns
- Any other defining demographics
  - Leverage this segmentation to recruit and motivate evangelist groups

EVANGELIST PROGRAM
EXECUTION

Build microsite with registration engine

- Send e-mail invitations to recruit participants
  - Invitations will map to segments developed through database analysis
- Send ongoing e-mails to activate participants
  - Potentially a monthly newsletter or automated e-mails
- Report regularly on key metrics
  - Individual referrals and high-value patterns
  - Total referrals
  - Success of activation efforts
- Alter program structure to optimize ROI

VIRAL PROGRAM

- Launch a viral campaign among consumers using a mix of online and guerilla tactics
  - Outdoor events/street teams

- Microsite
- Viral e-mail
- Engage consumers in an entertaining, unexpected way to build awareness and to encourage them to "pay it forward" to friends and colleagues
    - Builds brand
    - Drives interest
    - Creates demand
- Outdoor giant (<u>icons of industry</u>), as for example: palm tree, island, sailboat, compass, hibiscus, etc.
    - Place giant inflatable (palm tree, island, sailboat, bottle of rum, compass, hibiscus—lifestyle icons) in opportunity markets
    - Deploy street teams with collateral to drive awareness and get free trial sign-ups
- _____ Microsite
    - "(Insert company name here) TV commercial" mockumentary
    - A short documentary piece that profiles the long-fabled _____, their mission to island lifestyle everywhere
    - (Insert company name here)-mail
    - Create customizable branded e-mail site featuring the island lifestyle icons

VIRAL DISTRIBUTION

- There are two approaches we can take to propagate. The first is organic propagation
    - Leverage existing relationships—customers, vendors, employees
    - Use free distribution outlets
        - Send e-mails to all registered (insert company name here) customers and prospects
        - Send similar e-mails to "friends and family" for viral propagation
        - Employees should be encouraged to distribute to personal/professional networks

- Video distribution
  - Post on YouTube/iFilm/Yahoo!/Google
  - Push for coverage on VH1's Web Junk
  - Push to the ad blogs (i.e.: AdRants, AdFreak, AdAge)
  - Leverage through measured PR efforts

- The second is active seeding
  - Support distribution with a paid seeding effort, actively promoting the videos in key Web channels that have historically supported viral dissemination through free and paid placements
  - Paid seeding campaign specifics
    - Identify and work with influencers among key audiences as well as general interest sites/bloggers to feature, discuss, and disseminate the videos
    - Support free distribution with paid placement on blogs and video sites
    - Work with participants in forums to develop interest
    - E-mail blast to select third-party lists

(Lifestyle icons) promotion

- Large-scale inflatable island lifestyle icons will be strategically placed in heavily trafficked, targeted locations in fifteen cities, three days per city, on a rotating basis
- Accompanying the island lifestyle icons will be brand ambassadors, who will promote the product and hand out promotional materials to drive interested consumers to a microsite
  - Also deploy wireless credit card readers to capture orders on the spot
- It is anticipated that these street team events will have direct impact on several thousand people per event day with ten thousand-plus being exposed to our footprint, branding, and signage

- Once at the microsite, there will be additional tactics to further interest and drive trials

Search engine marketing

- We recommend leveraging promotional concepts and creative in a portion of (insert company name here)'s current search campaign to support an overarching, integrated presence
- To this end, creative executions would be developed to leverage viral concepts against targeted keyword opportunities
  - Brand keywords
  - Keywords directly related to creative executions
- Additional search engine marketing executions will be focused on driving acquisition as well as creating synergies with other campaign elements
- This synergy will support the buzz factor generated by TV advertising and help energize the viral elements

TV/radio overview

- Assume heavier spending early in the starting quarter to increase awareness of the new creative
- Identify current best performance direct response media as measured by cost per customer metrics
- Consider "passion buys" such as "Golf Networks" and "Bloomberg"

Online overview

- Advertise in Web sites that have a high composition of the target audience
- Further, reinforce the media buy through placements that align closely with the psychographics of the target audience
- Deploy highly visible "teaser" ad units during the evangelist/ viral phase of the campaign
  - Creative executions to have minimal branding during this phase

- Utilize extremely high-visible and high-impact advertising placements to coincide with the launch of broadcast media
  - Rich media units, roadblocks
- Sustain the buy through a variety of ad units to generate a steady flow of inquiries for the _____ offering
- Optimize the buy continually to garner maximum return on investment

Viral program

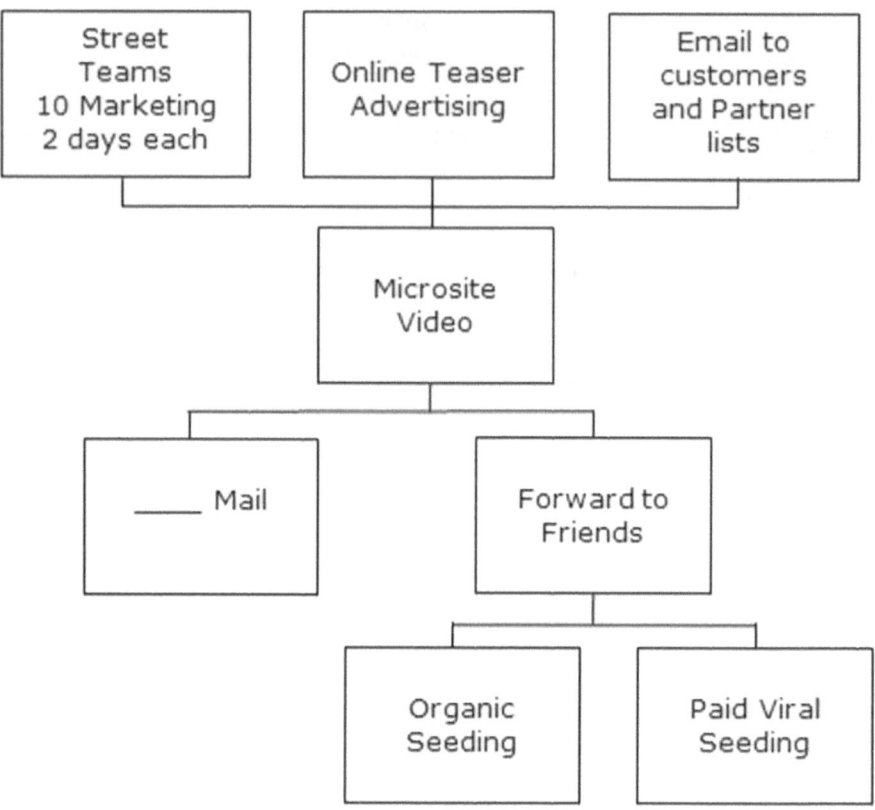

Metrics and measurement

- Program will be evaluated on the following criteria
  - Total e-mails sent by message and audience
  - Total CTR on e-mails
  - Total unique visits
  - Point of origin for visits—street team cards, online media, search, e-mail, etc.
  - Promotion registrations
  - Forward to a friend
  - Forward to a friend responses
  - Response to sign-up e-mail sent out fifteen days prior to free trial ending

- Registrants pushed into the long-term leads pool
- Number of street team cards distributed
- Free trial
- Conversion

- **Web Site Kickoff Meeting Agenda**
- **Web Site Specifications for a Bid**
- **Proposal for Building a Web Site**
- **Web Site Outline Approval Form**

WEB SITE KICKOFF MEETING AGENDA:

- Familiarizing them with (insert your company here) and what the company does
- Reviewing (insert your company here) competition
- Going over competitive analysis
- Discussion of deliverables
- Understanding the creative expectations
- Evaluating the existing Web site and brand

Web Site Specifications

Before a quote to build a Web site can be given, the following specifications are needed.

Web Technology
- What are the current technologies?
Ex: HTML, XML, CSS, JavaScript, PHP, MySQL, etc.

- Any additional open source or proprietary content systems being used?
Ex: the PR and Investor portal.

- Do you wish to continue using existing technologies?

Scope of Sites
- Four sites found for various offices, subsidiaries, PR portal, etc. Will all of these be part of the reskin?

Static or Dynamic Structures
- Will we be building dynamic page layout structures for reusability and scalability, or static pages?
Ex: dynamic structures for page layout, default variables, headers, navigation, footers, etc.

Database
- Will there be any changes or integrations to an existing database?
- Any expectations for database-driven content management capabilities?
- Existing reports or reporting capabilities?

Integration and Documentation
- Will we need to integrate the final changes into an existing hosting solution or just deliver the final code?
- Does the client need additional optimized migration services such as search engine safe page redirects for old URL requests?
- Will the client need documentation for the code produced?

Thanks,

(Insert your company name here)

Morgan D. Rees

PROPOSAL FOR BUILDING A WEB SITE

SITUATION APPRAISAL

- (Insert your company name here) is planning on revamping the general look and feel of the company in a phased approach. This rebranding effort will include the design of the corporate identity system using new logo to be delivered by the client, company Web site, print collateral, as well as all means of marketing and brand communications, including a PowerPoint presentation template and tradeshow graphics.

OBJECTIVES

In order to assist (insert your company name here) with the revamp of its corporate brand we recommend the following projects:

Corporate identity system package, which includes the design of the corporate identity system, including business card, letterhead, #10 envelope, and label design.

Web site package, which includes assisting (insert your company name here) in the development of an information architecture wire frame for the home page as well as a review of the Web site map and navigation, design of the home page and one inside page template, production of a short, small flash limited to three message loops as well as the development of the entire Web site.

Collateral package, which includes the design, development, and art production of a presentation folder, a booklet-style eight-page brochure with a pocket in the back, a two-page data sheet template design and production of a total of seven data sheets.

PowerPoint package, which includes the design of a PowerPoint template including a title slide and a master slide.

Library of icons package, which includes the design and development of a total of _ industry icons to be used throughout the package.

PROCESS

At (insert your Web design firm name here), we believe that in order to effectively achieve the above-mentioned goals, the following steps should be taken and followed:

Discovery
(Insert your Web design firm name here) will conduct an initial interview in order to become familiar with (insert your company name here) and all of its products/services offerings. During this meeting we will explore the company's vision, respective target audience, and review the company's existing brand. We will discuss the corporate brand message as well as examine all relevant competitors' materials. We will explore the overall objective and establish the design/image criteria and the vision for the future of the company. During the discovery phase we will interview the stakeholders, audit the existing materials, and analyze the competition depending on (insert your company name here)'s needs. We need the key executive/decision-makers to be present for this meeting.

Internal Research
To accompany the results from our discovery phase, (insert your Web design firm name here) will also conduct internal research that will study (insert your company name here) and its competition. We will gather information through an internal visual audit and evaluate (insert your company name here) and its competitors' existing materials. This evaluation will include a review of all print as well as online communications.

Strategy and Analysis
When sufficient information has been gathered, objectives have been identified, internal research has been conducted, and all insights have been agreed upon, we will have an understanding of how and where (insert your company name here) is positioned today and where it wants to be in the future. (Insert your Web design firm name here) will

then recommend a wire frame for the Web site home page information architecture as well as a list of recommended print collateral to be designed and developed within the original estimate provided.

PROCESS

Design

Once the recommended approach has been agreed upon and the specific projects identified, (insert your Web design firm name here)'s entire creative team will be assigned to each individual project. Utilizing the strategy, which has been driven from our discovery and internal research phase, our team will generate a range of design directions (minimum of five initial concepts) that (insert your company name here) can select from. We will then narrow down the selection to one design direction and will go through two rounds of minor changes to the design based on our standard pricing to finalize the design.

Development

Once the design has been finalized, our production team makes the designed vision a reality by producing it accurately and efficiently. The development phase includes the time it takes for the production of the final approved design, which includes typesetting and electronic file production. We deliver projects in several phases. For print material we deliver print-ready master files of the final designs that are ready for production and can be used as templates for the internal team to expand upon.

For Web site projects we either deliver master electronic files of the designs in Photoshop format that are ready for production, or we take the project all the way to completion by slicing the files and handling all front- and back-end programming.

Delivery

All projects at (insert your Web design firm name here) undergo internal and external quality control in order to assure both design and technical accuracy.

MISCELLANEOUS SERVICES

Art Direction
We will provide art direction in the cases where the client selects to work with an illustrator or commission an artist for a specific requirement.
N/A

Photo Direction
Our pricing includes selection of three to five images from online resources for usage on the entire project.
Included are:
Copywriting
We offer copywriting services through a pool of preferred copywriters. You may review their sample work and work with them directly once you find the appropriate copywriter.

GENERAL ASSUMPTIONS

Deliverables
(Insert your Web design firm name here) will deliver electronic files of the final designs to the client.

Assumptions
(Insert your Web design firm name here) will be designing the corporate brand package for (insert your company name here) based on input and comments from our initial research and strategy consultation. Please keep in mind all pricing does not include creation of any charts, graphs, or icons other than the ones specified within the proposal.

Staging Server
All initial concepts and designs will reside on (insert your Web design firm name here)'s server up to final design approval stage. The Web site is to be fully developed on the client's dedicated server upon approval of the template designs.

Rights Transferred
(Insert your Web design firm name here) to transfer all rights to the final approved files upon full payment received from (insert your company name here).

Photography/Illustration
All stock imagery that has been selected by (insert your Web design firm name here) to be purchased directly by the client.

PRICING

Discovery
Initial Interviews
Internal Research

Strategy and Analysis
Web site Wire Frame and Site Map development

Design
Project Management

Corporate identity system package, which includes the design of the corporate identity system including business card, letterhead, #10 envelope, and label design.

Web site package, which includes assisting (insert your company name here) in the development of an information architecture wire frame for the home page as well as a review of the Web site map and navigation, design of the home page and one inside page template, production of a short, small flash limited to three message loops as well as the development of the entire Web site.

Design

Development (Programming)
Based upon an NT based CMS package with a total of one hundred pages, in English only.

Delivery (Quality and compatibility control)

Collateral package, which includes the design, development, and art production of a booklet-style eight-page brochure/folder with a pocket in the back, a two-page data sheet template design, and production of a total of seven data sheets.

Total:
Client Approval: _____

Please keep in mind our pricing does not include creation of any charts, graphs, or any icons other than the ones specified above. Any third party licenses to be purchased directly by the client and all training and support, if required, to be quoted separately.

TIME LINE

Corporate identity system package, which includes the design of the corporate identity system including business card, letterhead, #10 envelope, and a label design.

Web site package, which includes assisting (insert your company name here) in the development of an information architecture wire frame for the home page as well as a review of the Web site map and navigation, design of the home page and one inside page template, production of a short, small flash limited to three message loops as well as the development of the entire Web site.

Design

Development (Programming)
In CMS based on total of one hundred pages in English only.

Delivery (Quality and compatibility control)

Collateral package, which includes the design, development, and art production of a booklet-style eight-page brochure/folder with a pocket in the back, a two-page data sheet template design, and production of a total of seven data sheets. Please keep in mind majority of the projects could be worked on simultaneously.

PAYMENT TERMS

Creative

Discovery, strategy, and analysis as well as design for all projects.

Development of the Web site

Total for all projects

Retainer
Fifty percent of the creative cost to be paid up front as a retainer, and the balance to be paid upon completion of each project. One third of the development cost to be paid as a retainer, and the balance in two payments based on progress.

Total Retainer for all projects:

Final payments

Final balance on discovery, strategy, and analysis to be paid upon completion.

Final balance on project management to be paid upon completion of all projects.

Final balance on corporate identity package to be paid upon completion.

Final balance on design of the Web site to be paid upon completion.

Final balance on design of the collateral to be paid upon completion.

Second payment on the development of the Web site upon review of the alpha version of the Web site.

Third and final payment on the development of the Web site upon completion and final delivery of the Web site.

Client Approval: _____

WEB SITE OUTLINE APPROVAL FORM

I hereby confirm that I have reviewed and approve the site map and wire frame/information architecture attached that has been developed by (insert your Web design firm name here) for the (insert your company name here) corporate Web site. (Insert your Web design firm name here) can proceed with the creative process and begin generating designs based upon the approved wire frame.

_____

Approval signature on Behalf of (insert your company name here)

SITE MAP: (Insert your company name here)

Home Page Overview

The home page will play a highly strategic role in setting the tone of the overall site experience. As the primary gateway to the site's offerings, the home page must quickly and powerfully capture the essence of the (insert your company name here) brand / key messaging while guiding site visitors from targeted audience groups to the highest priority site content and features.

Home page elements to include:
1. Firm Identity and messaging
2. Web site Global Navigation
3. Photo Pathway (Motion based element highlighting outstanding photography of images that convey (insert your company name here) brand message)
4. Pathway for "(insert your company name here) University"
5. Pathway for "Intern Program/ (insert your company name here) Foundation"
6. Rotating logos of "Certifications"
7. Rotating logos of "Customers"

8. An area with direct access to (insert your company name here) service offering based on the verticals.

9. News and Events area

Footer

This represents the common elements that will appear at the bottom of every page of the Web site.

© 20_ _ (insert your company name here) All Rights Reserved.

Global Navigation (Primary)

1. (Insert lead product or service): This section will offer up a background on (insert your company name here) and our philosophy and how it would benefit our customers.

2. (Insert company solutions or practices): This section will offer up an overview of (insert your company name here) solution or service offerings based on the vertical markets. Once clicked on to the solution or service page it will take you to the "Overview" page. On this page there will be general information and overview of (insert your company name here) offerings.

Second-Level Navigation:

- Second-Tier Services—There will be access to (insert your company name here) solutions for the financial services markets, and on the side of the page we will link into case studies that would support our offering.

- Second-Tier Services—There will be access to (insert your company name here) solutions for the _____ markets, and on the side of the page we will links into case studies that would support our offering.

- Second-Tier Services—There will be access to (insert your company name here) solutions for the _____ markets, and on the side of the page we will link into case studies that would support our offering.

- Second-Tier Services—There will be access to (insert your company name here) solutions for the _____ markets, and on the side of the page we will link into case studies that would support our offering.
- Second-Tier Services—There will be access to (insert your company name here) solutions for the _____ markets, and on the side of the page we will link into case studies that would support our offering.
- Second-Tier Services—There will be access to (insert your company name here) solutions for the _____ markets, and on the side of the page we will link into case studies that would support our offering.

3. Products: This section will offer up a summary of the firm's products. You have case studies of specific products and can provide clients case study PDF downloads on the side margins on this page.

4. Global Reach: This section will cover the firm's service offerings.

5. Product Offerings: This section will cover our existing product offering. We will start with an Overview page which will cover our expertise and years of experience and therefore predeveloped, existing products

Second-Level Navigation:
- Product 1—There will be access to (insert your company name here) Product 1 legacy product and how you will continue supporting the product and will integrate this product with other products to create tailored solutions for your customers.
- Product 2—There will be access to (insert your company name here) Product 2 and again more information on your support for the product.

6. About Us
Second-Level Navigation:
- Management—There will be bios of the management team.
  B of D—There will be bios on the board of directors.

7. Newsroom
Second=Level Navigation:
- Press Releases—There will be a list of our latest press releases, and once you click on them the detail press release.
  Events—There will be a list of events we are attending.

8. Investor Relations

<u>Global Navigation (Secondary)</u>
1. Home
2. Contact Us

MARKETING PROGRAMS, COMPONENTS AND PROCESS

Sales depend on marketing to provide sales leads. The CEO depends on marketing to build the company brand. But what does marketing depend on to fulfill these obligations? Marketing programs.

Marketing programs are imperative to generating demand and evoking direct response from customers. They also create interest in your company—especially important during a down and competitive economy. Marketing programs should support the brand image and personality and fight for mind share.

Still, even the best marketing programs are destined to fail without first determining the correct process for operating them. Day-to-day work is difficult enough as it is—programs with proper structure will run more smoothly, drive productivity, reduce time-to-market, and increase revenue.

Marketing programs make your company look exciting, exuberant, and alive. People want to work and buy products from companies like that.

Included in this chapter:
- The War Room and Real-Time Processes
- Investor Relations
  - Templates
    - IR Process Flow
- Sales

- - The Inside Sales Process
  - Templates
    - Collateral Status at a Glance
- Marketing Materials
  - Templates
    - Process Flow
    - Permission Marketing Flow
    - Sign-Off Sheet
    - Order Form for Sales
- Quality Assurance
  - Strategy
  - Templates
    - QA Forms & Design
    - Sieve Overview
- Customer Retention
  - Frequent Users Club
  - Volume Incentive Program

THE WAR ROOM AND REAL-TIME PROCESSES

During the height of the dotcom frenzy, the concept of Internet time became popular. Internet time dictated that companies could be born, teams formed, products developed, markets made, and fortunes gained in far less time than ever before. Today, while Internet time has largely been dismissed as a figment of entrepreneurial imagination, it has been replaced with the far more realistic concepts of how a company can operate in real time to the delight of satisfied customers.

In today's market economy, attention spans are longer than during the dotcom bubble. Venture capitalists conduct far more due diligence prior to investing in a start-up company. In fact, venture capital investments in start-up companies were down 60 percent and the vast majority of investments were concentrated on backing existing companies. This means that the successful start-up is not the company that can spend its venture capital investments at the fastest pace. Rather, the race goes to the company that can conserve cash without abandoning execution. Such companies spend more time planning and perfecting their innovations, honing business strategies, identifying target markets, developing management teams, and addressing and meeting customer expectations.

The increase in the collective attention span does not mean that emerging companies are working at a slower pace. It means that customers can be more selective, demanding more performance, additional features, better service, and more attractive pricing—all factors that increase the need for heightened productivity. It means that the successful start-up must mature faster than ever before, by adapting the processes formerly associated with larger, more established companies. It means that various departments of the company must operate interdependently in real time.

Companies that succeed in this new era will be those that invest in real-time systems to adapt to changing circumstances, make decisions without hesitating, and address customer expectations without delay. Building the real-time organization requires the full commitment of everyone in the company, from top managers and the rank-and-file employees. Everyone must understand the importance of real-time operations. Processes that formerly may have taken months to filter down through multiple layers of management must be understood and adopted in the course of a single meeting. Real-time operations defy the hierarchical management chain. The CEO and the software engineer must drink from the same fire hose, with the shared understanding that they are committed to a larger goal - the satisfaction of customers that, paradoxically, are harder to satisfy than ever before.

THE "WAR ROOM"

The success of real-time processes rely on the "War Room," where executives, managers, and employees at every level of the company meet to discuss customer issues and requests, product development requirements, third-party integration requirements, bug lists, and the myriad details that go into a complex technology product. The War Room is a face-to-face interaction with up-to-the-minute status reports to track progress, remove obstacles, and identify and resolve problems in order to ensure that even the most aggressive development and marketing goals and key milestones are met. War Room meetings are intense and demanding. What enhancements is the customer requesting, and how fast can we deliver them? What fixes need to be made, and who's responsible? What are the customer's objections and how can we respond? What will it take to close the sale?

"Whose action item is it?" is the mantra for War Room meetings, with the responsibility owned by accountable individuals with the understanding that they will get the support they need from every department and team in the company. Market requirements plans, bug and feature tracking systems, product release schedules, customer support, and presale and post sale processes can all be managed from the War Room environment. Instead of pushing paper from department to department, the War Room infuses the company with the human element of real-time accountability and stand-up behavior.

A PERVASIVE SENSE OF URGENCY

When team members share the understanding that a customer problem is expected to be resolved by the end of the day versus by the next product release, the sense of urgency becomes pervasive throughout the entire company and fosters a corporate culture that recognizes and rewards individual initiative, teamwork, and risk taking. Several timeworn axioms apply, including "when in doubt, make a decision" and "lead, follow, or get out of the way."

Software patches or hardware integration issues get solved in minutes instead of weeks. When everyone is in the same room and on the same page, voice mail gets answered and e-mail requests get attention. So long as an issue stays on the War Room agenda, it remains exceedingly difficult to ignore the problem, to get too busy, or to shunt responsibility. The entire team becomes mutually and collectively accountable, or individuals risk becoming the butt of humorous, albeit pointed, attention.

It is vital to integrate sales programs with the War Room's real-time processes. Initially raw leads generated through mailings to target lists, marketing campaigns, trade shows and seminars, VAR databases, Web marketing, media coverage, and other marketing vehicles require focus on overarching marketing goals. As leads are generated by marketing activities, outbound telesales, direct sales activities, and other means, the focus moves to tracking the prospect's progress through the sales funnel.

Live contact with the prospect requires confirmation and tracking of the source of the lead, the prospect's level of interest, receipt of product information, and assignment to the appropriate sales representative or channel partner. Initial meetings determine key buyers, potential competition, needs, and pain points. Presales engineers are assigned, success criteria are documented, and an evaluation plan is established. Evaluation units are shipped and configured, customer support staff is assigned, and success criteria are reconfirmed. As the prospect becomes an active sales lead, the account's needs are met, pricing is negotiated, specific projects are noted, including time frames, budgets, and requirements, and key contacts and decision-makers are identified. Qualified leads become part of sales projections and the focal point of sales-driven War Room meetings.

For complex technology products, the sales proposition typically proceeds across a multistage process, consisting of a good story, an enticing trial, an established trust and competency, a demonstration of the value proposition, and proof or validation of the value proposition. The War Room surfaces any issues regarding the prospect account's status in the sales process.

In today's marketplace, customers can be decidedly reluctant to adopt products from an emerging company. The company's product road map, the planned products and services that the company will deliver over a twelve- to eight-month time frame, becomes an important vehicle in reinforcing the perception that the company is committed to serving the customer across the long haul. The product road map combines marketing's vision, creativity, and understanding of market segments and competitive offerings; sales' first-hand knowledge of customer needs; engineering's knowledge of the technologies that can be applied to the required solutions; and everyone's commitment. The War Room becomes the focal point for the critical decision-making process regarding the definition of the product road map and its invariable refinement as marketing, sales, and engineering engage in the discussion. Opinions invariably clash and sparks may fly, but these sparks illuminate the way forward.

Although the sales organization ultimately owns the customer relationship, each employee, in every functional discipline, must be aware of his/her impact on formulating customer perception and shaping the company's image in the minds of target customers. The War Room helps to anticipate the invariable "aches and pains" that accompany the introduction of a new product and to proactively deal with issues before they become real problems with the company. "We're about to lose this account" becomes a battle cry that rallies the entire company. The confirmation of sales wins, successful installations, and the referencing of an account as a satisfied customer are cause for celebration. Although Internet time and high burn rates are relics of the bubble, real-time processes translate to revenues, profits, and long-term viability for the emerging company.

# # # #

INVESTOR RELATIONS

INVESTOR RELATIONS PROCESS FLOW

(Designation of teams; assignment of responsibilities)

Activity Flow	Responsible Team (*= To take Action)
1. Determine Budget Location	IRA / MC
2. Complete Project Definition or request funds transfer	IRA / MC (local budget) Region
3. Develop Creative Platform/Project Briefing	IRA
4. Determine IR involvement/IR Strategy	IRA / MC / CEO
5. Schedule Premeeting	IRA / MC
• Complete Worksheets	
1) Choose response mechanism	
2) Identify pieces (may include data sheet)	
• Determine use of various media options	IRA / MC
1) Road Show	
2) Internet	
3) White Paper	
4) Special Event	
6. Complete input form:	IRA
7. Quotes from Vendors (may need various options)	MC
8. Select Vendor	MC
9. Initiate Purchase Req./: Required on vendor quote:	MC (local budget)
• Budget number, Ship-to location with quantity, Delivery date	MC (cc of request to COO)
9a. Initiate Purchase Req.	
Shipping Instructions to Vendor	
10. Production	MC
Project Status and Approvals	
✓ Project Status Meeting (Weekly)	MC / IRA / CEO
✓ Production Proof Approvals (ongoing)	MC
✓ Formal Approval Cycle (s) per Marketing Process	MC
• Marcom, Marketing, Legal	

11. Signoff form	IRA / MC / CTO / L / CEO
11a. Measurement/Results/Feedback	IRA / MC
12. Close Out Event/Activity Folder After Receipt	MC

MC = Marketing, IR Agency: CTO, CEO, L = Legal

SALES

The Inside Sales Process

Collateral Status at a Glance

The Inside Sales Process

Inside Sales

Policies and Procedures/Workflows

Last Revised	07/09/_ _	Name	Signature
Approved	SVP of Marketing		
Approved	Director of Sales		
Approved	COO		

CONTENTS

1. Introduction

1.1 Overview

The inside sales (IS) team is the front-line evangelist and extension of (insert your company name here) external sales organization. Inside sales is chartered with:

1. Evangelizing (insert your company name here) and (insert your company name here) products and services
2. Creating, identifying, and qualifying leads for external sales.

For inside sales to be successful, every inside sales representative (ISR) must be committed to the company's mission and objectives, immediately familiar with the company's branding and messaging, and have in-depth knowledge of (insert your company name here)'s value proposition as well as the relative product benefits and features.

The ISR must identify and then qualify a prospective customer through direct contact over the phone. It is imperative that each lead be contacted directly by IS to (1) introduce (insert your company name here) and its products; (2) determine the appropriate contacts/ decision-makers; (3) obtain other relevant qualifying information for external sales. The ISR is expected to manage their schedule and priorities effectively to achieve the designated inside sales bogey/targets noted in Section 1.3. In addition, open and constant communication between inside sales and external sales is required to ensure a smooth "handoff" of qualified leads and productive prospecting by the entire sales organization.

1.2 INSIDE SALES REPRESENTATIVE (ISR) RESPONSIBILITIES

- Exceed 100 percent of quota for assigned regions
- Current on (insert your company name here) products/services, the company in general, and competitive landscape
- Understand all current and planned lead generation programs
- Understand all current lead collection tools and processes
- High level of proficiency in automation tools to manage workflow (lead collection and SF db)
- Understand current targeted accounts (target lists and other raw leads) and relative priorities
- Maximize the use of leads generated from all sources to achieve quota
- Develop working relationships and understand lead/account priorities within each region supported
- Consistent communication with field reps and active time management to achieve quota
- Continuous transition of QLs (appointment) to field reps and assistance in penetration of other targeted suspects
- Coordinate day-to-day account issues and strategies with ASEs
- Elevate relevant issues/exceptions to sales operations manager and regional directors
- Continuous identification of new leads and development into qualified leads/appointments
- Current on all (insert your company name here) literature, company policies, price lists, and objectives
- Accurate and timely maintenance of data/account notes via lead collection and SF.com db
- Honest, accurate, and timely reporting of all trackers, status reports, and other administration as defined
- Active and effective time management so as to achieve quota and the targets noted below

1.3 INSIDE SALES TARGETS / BOGEYS

INSIDE SALES TARGETS
25+ Outbound Calls / day
25 Suspects / week
15 Prospects / week
5 QLs/Appointments / week
QLs = Qualified Leads

1.4 (INSERT YOUR COMPANY NAME HERE) NORTH AMERICA SALES TERRITORY MAP

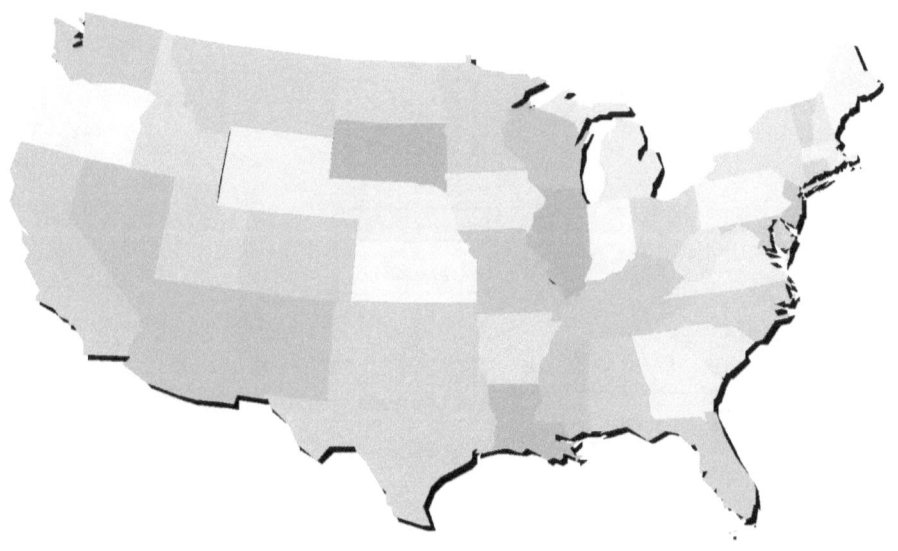

1.5 (INSERT YOUR COMPANY NAME HERE) SALES TERRITORY BREAKDOWN BY STATE

Notes:

ASE = Account Sales Executives
ISR = Inside Sales Rep

2. LEAD MANAGEMENT

2.1 "HIGH-LEVEL" LEAD COLLECTION WORKFLOW

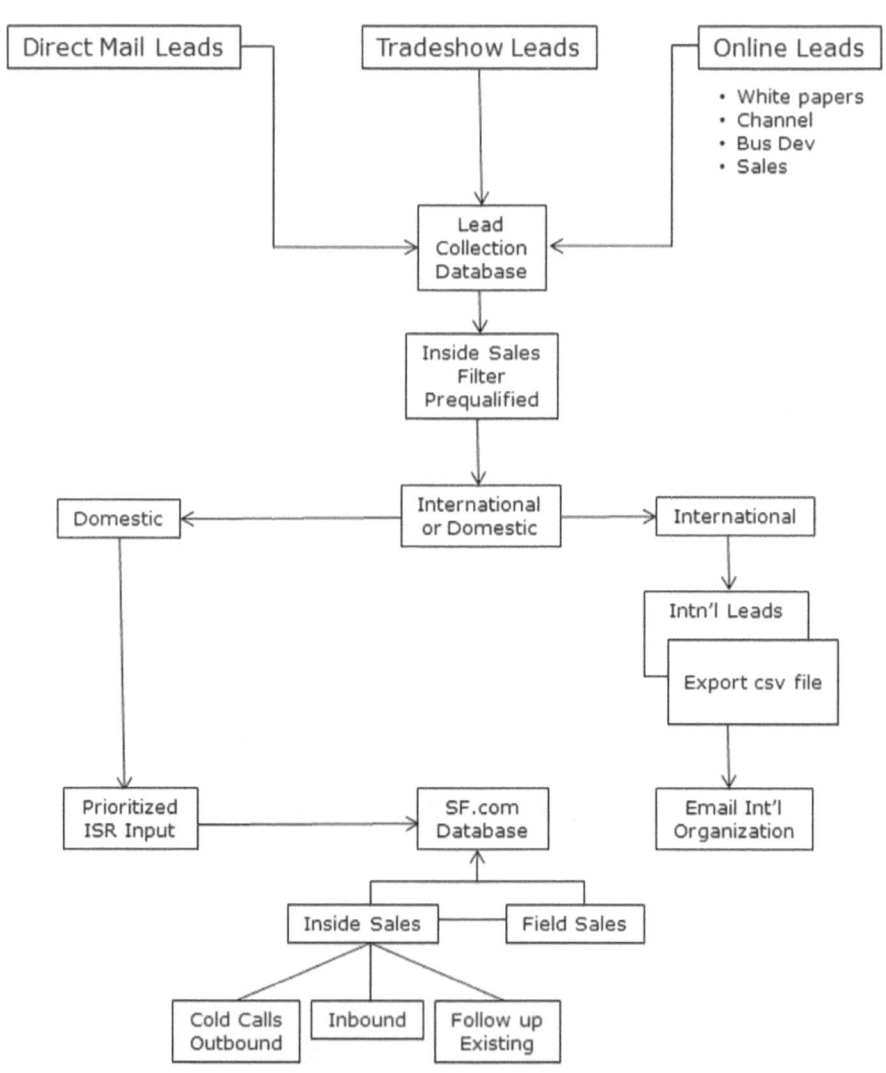

2.2 LEAD COLLECTION WALKTHROUGH

STEP	ACTIVITY
GENERAL	Leads are collected from a variety of sources. Prior to the establishment of the inside sales organization, raw leads were worked and entered into SF.com by the account sales executives as required. The majority of those leads continue to be worked by the account sales executive. ASE generated leads will *not* be worked by ISRs unless identified by the ASE as a priority where inside support is required. This will help to maximize sales productivity and reduce the risk of a redundancy of efforts.
1	All marketing generated leads flow daily into the lead collection database, LCD (Leads Collected Database): • Online Leads (white paper, channel, Bus Dev, Sales) • Trade show leads • Direct mail leads
2	Inside sales reps access LCD and conduct filtering and qualifying procedures as outlined in Sections 2.5–2.7.
3	ISRs access the LCD: password: (Insert your company name here)
4	Determination is made. Is it the Americas or international?
4A	International leads are exported to a .csv file, which is e-mailed to the international sales team periodically (daily if volume requires).
4B	Domestic leads db will be prioritized daily and direct calls by the ISR initiated.
5	Lead input in SF.com by ISR and activities/tasks, call details, and other relevant qualifying information tracked via SF.com.

6	Other leads referred by ASE for existing follow-up will be accessed via SF.com and tracked similarly as in Step 5. ISR will input into SF.com if necessary. In cases where leads referred by ASEs have already been entered within SF.com, data integrity will be determined and updates entered as appropriate by the ISR.
7	Inbound direct call leads and leads generated by ISRs will not be collected in LCD, but will be tracked directly in SF.com (as in Step 5) above.

2.3 CURRENT STATE PROCESS: SALES ACTIVITY TRACKING—EXTERNAL SALES

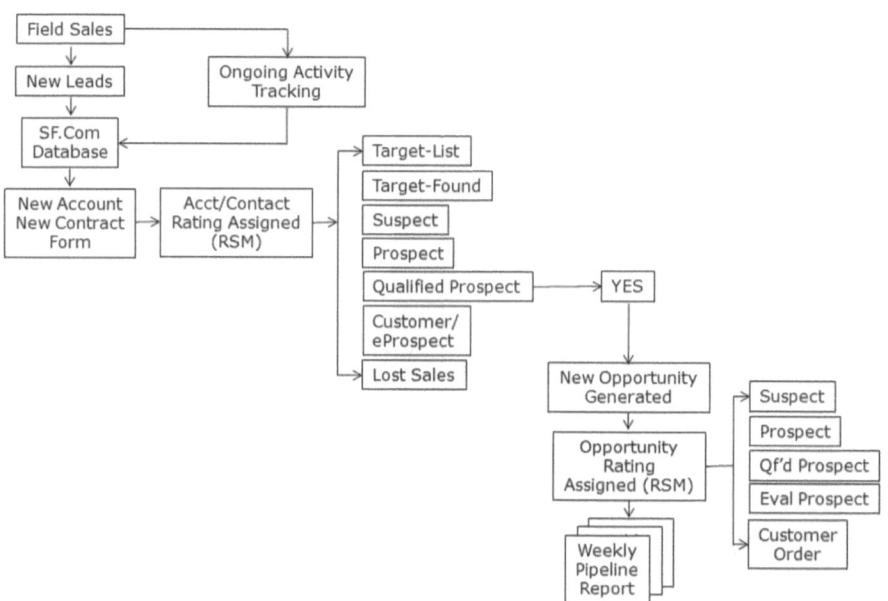

2.4 SALES ACTIVITY TRACKING—EXTERNAL SALES— WALKTHROUGH

STEP	ACTIVITY
GENERAL	Although there will be slight variations among individual ASEs as to the timing and manner in which they process and input raw leads in SF.com, the current process in general for account sales executives generated leads/activity tracking is flow charted in Section 2.3. The workflow and corresponding activities are documented here to ensure:

- Inside sales has a clear understanding of current lead and presales activity tracking conducted by external sales.
- A smooth transition between inside and external sales upon hand-off of qualified leads.

1A	Account sales executives enter new leads at the appropriate time into SF.com and note any relevant qualifying information.
1B	Existing leads previously entered as well as leads that have progressed further down the sales cycle are tracked as on-going activity via SF.com.
2	New leads inputted by ASEs are entered via the "New Account" form and/ or the "New Contact" form in SF.
3	ASE assigns an "Account Rating" and/or "Contact Rating" as appropriate (Target-List, Target-Found, Suspect, Prospect, Qualified Prospect, Customer/e-Prospect, Lost Sale).
4	Once lead has progressed to the "Qualified Prospect" stage and represents a "realistic" opportunity, ASE generates a "New Opportunity" in SF. Multiple opportunities can then be generated by the ASE per account/contact as appropriate.
5	ASE assigns an "Opportunity Rating" as appropriate (Suspect, Prospect, Qfd Prospect, Customer, Order).
6	ASE generates activity reports and sends weekly status to Corp. HQ.

NOTES:

* Required fields in Account, Contact, and Opportunity forms in SF are highlighted in red color.

** SF = SF.com or Salesforce.com database

2.5 PROPOSED "LIFE OF LEAD"

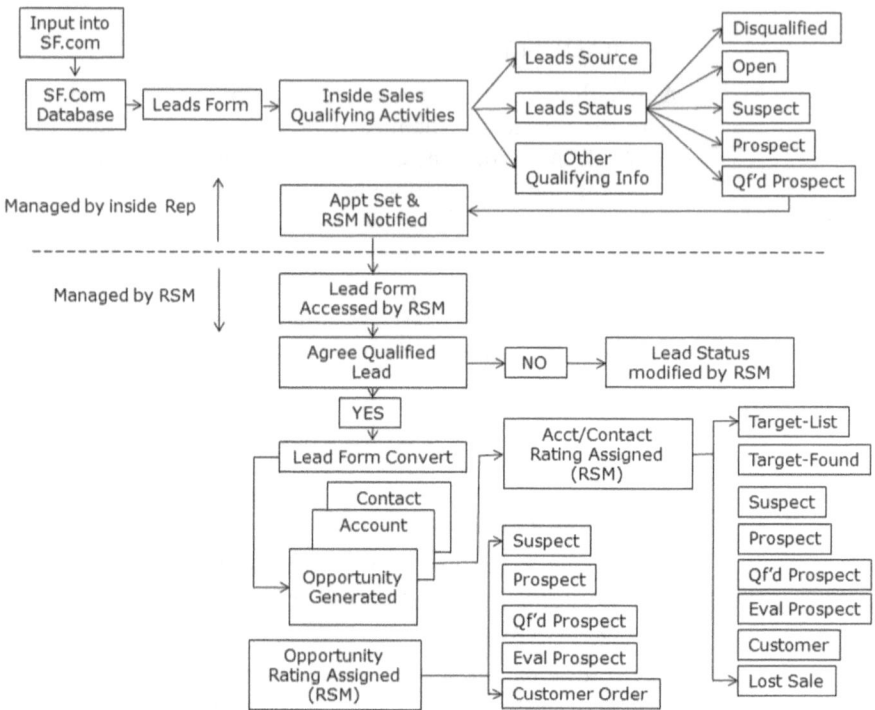

2.6 "Life of Lead" Walkthrough

STEP	ACTIVITY
GENERAL	The process outlined in Section 2.5 represents the "proposed Life of Lead" post the establishment of the inside sales organization. The activities ABOVE THE (DASHED) line represent those managed and owned by inside sales. Activities BELOW THE LINE represent account sales executives ownership.

Account sales executives generated leads will continue to be tracked by account sales executives via their current sales activity tracking—external (Sections 2.3 and 2.4)—unless flagged and identified as a priority where inside sales support is required. If inside sales support is required, lead will be tracked as outlined in Section 2.6 "Life of Lead Walkthrough" (step 2C).

1	Leads are collected from a variety of sources per Sections 2.1 and 2.2.

2A	Leads collected from all sources (for domestic) are prioritized per the lead prioritization chart noted in Section 2.7.

Inbound call leads will always take precedence over every other lead. This is based on the usually high level of interest from these types of leads. Also, any *hot* marketing generated leads (i.e., trade shows) also take priority. On most days the ISR will not have *hot* leads available to them. In these cases, the lead prioritization chart is still used (Section 2.7) from row B on down.

2B	Row B leads: LCD (lead collection database) will be checked each morning by ISRs. Any leads downloaded into the LCD from prior days will be processed first. *Warm* marketing leads will also be followed up on at this time.

2C	Row C leads: ISR will check in with their ASEs each day to see if there are any high-priority leads that require ISR follow-up and a direct call.

These ASE generated leads will be in the SF database. The ISR will also make all their follow-up calls scheduled for the day. The ISR will be calling as many existing leads as possible during the day. Any *cool* generated marketing leads will be followed up at this time as well.

2D	Time permitting daily, ISRs will process any first-time cold calling off target lists or any other cold lead.
3	Once leads have been identified and prioritized per steps 1-5, ISRs will manually input raw lead into SF.com database using the "New Lead" Form.
	Note: This will help to isolate activities conducted by inside sales and account sales executives since account sales executives are primarily using the Accounts and Contacts Forms to track their generated leads as outlined in Sections 2.3 and 2.4.
4A	Calls are initiated for those leads inputted into SF.com and any relevant follow-up activities/tasks, call details and other relevant qualifying information noted using the "Lead Form."
4B	If there is an existing record in SF.com for the lead, the ISR must contact the respective ASE for an update/clarification before proceeding.
	See General section from above for data entry of leads generated from field sales reps.
4C	Data integrity will be validated when speaking with the contact at each lead. All contact information will be verified (i.e., contact name, address, office/cell phone, etc.). Ensure "Lead Status" / "Rating" is correct.

2.7 LEAD PRIORITIZATION TABLE

A Inbound Sales Calls; ASAP ASE leads
Hot—Marketing, Channel, Bus. Dev., and Field generated leads

B New lead
Warm—Marketing, Channel, Bus. Dev., and Field generated leads

C Existing lead; Follow-Up Leads—Previously Scheduled Tasks; Existing SF ASE leads
Cool— - Marketing, Channel, Bus. Dev., and Field generated leads

D *Cold* Calls (Target List, etc.)

Hot—Immediate need; wants callback.
Warm—Wants more information.
Cool—No discernable information; literature fulfillment and follow-up.
Marketing Leads——Leads generated by specific marketing campaigns:
- Trade Show
- Online
- White Paper
- Direct Mail
- Target E-mail Blasts (purchased lists)
- *Channel Leads*—Leads generated by our channel/VAR partners.
- *Bus. Dev. Leads*—Leads generated by our bus. dev. department.
- *ASE Leads*—Leads generated by our account sales executives department.

2.8 INSIDE SALES REP (ISR) – DETAILED LEAD ENTRY PROCESS

STEPS	ACTIVITY
1	Log-on to SF.com database.
2	Press "New Lead" to enter a new lead.
3	Fill in as much qualifying information as possible obtained from research activities. REQUIRED fields are as follows:

    a. Last Name
    b. Company
    c. Lead Source—How did the contact hear about us?
    d. Lead Status—See below
    e. Area—What territory?
    f. Area Director—Who is the ASE?

Lead Status:
- Open—Default (i.e., no direct contact made)
- Suspect—Moderate interest
- Prospect—Identified two buying influencers; pain/need identified
- Qualified Lead—Face-to-face appointment made
- Disqualified—Contacted, and no current needs in the next nine months

4	Indicate the product of interest (Model #) for the lead from the following drop-down options:

    - Lease Package
    - Financial, Healthcare, Public Sector, etc.

5	Press "Save" button.
6	When making a call, press the "Log a Call" tab. A new window pops up.
7	Make the call.
8	If the target is not there leave a voice mail. Schedule a new call for later in the "Schedule follow up task" section. Indicate the "Status" as "Not Completed."
9	<u>If the target is there proceed as follows….</u>
10	If target is not the correct contact/decision-maker, get a new contact name and number. Replace current name with new name and number. Place a new call.

11   If the target is the correct contact/decision-maker proceed as follows:

12   Qualify and enter all appropriate notes.

13   If the target is not ready for a meeting (Suspect/Prospect) then schedule a follow-up call as outlined above.

14   Determine the "Lead Status" (see above).

15   Indicate new "Lead Status" by editing the record.

16   Send out sales e-mail and schedule to send out literature at the end of the day.

17   If the target is ready for a meeting proceed as follows....

18   Determine a time and date which works for both the prospect and ASE.

19   Press the "New Event" button. A new window pops up.

20   In the subject line indicate "Meeting" or "Call" for conference call.

21   Enter the "Date", "Time" and "Duration" of the meeting.

22   Paste your notes from the call over to the "Comments" field along with the address, contact name, and number.

23   Press "Invite Others." A new window pops up.

24   Select the appropriate ASE from the USER LIST and transfer them over to the INVITED USERS list.

25   Paste comments over in the "Comments" field as outlined above

26   Press "Send Invitation." The invitation will be sent via e-mail to both the ISR and ASE so that calendars may be noted.

27   Send a reminder e-mail to the prospect indicating the time and date of the meeting along with the ASE's contact number.

28   It is the ASE's responsibility to reschedule if needed.

29   For the lead record, "Lead form," indicate the "Lead Status" as "Qualified." Enter any additional information about the prospect obtained in the call.

30   If lead cannot be classified as "Qualified" based on information obtained, classify into one of the following ratings and follow up accordingly:
   • Open
   • Suspect
   • Prospect
   • Disqualified

2.9 Qualified Lead Hand-off and "Conversion"

BELOW THE LINE

STEPS	ACTIVITY
1	Once appointment for a face-to-face meeting w/ the lead has been set and the qualified lead is "Accepted" by the ASE, ASE will access lead via lead form and "CONVERT" lead into an opportunity by pressing the "Convert" button.
	ISRs should review appointment scheduled w/ ASEs during daily conference call and sync-up.
	Conversion automatically generates "New Opportunity" based on that lead as well as new "Account" and new "Contact." ASE will track activities and movement through sales from this point forward per Sections 2.3 and 2.4.
2	ISRs will *not* be permitted to "Convert" the record to an Opportunity/ ACCOUNT. This activity must be conducted by the ASE once qualified lead has been accepted.

NOTES

1. Inside reps are *not* authorized to create New Opportunities or to indicate a rating beyond Prospect. By the inside sales team working primarily in the "Lead Form" of SF.com, data integrity is maintained, ASEs can continue to track their activities in the same manner as the past, and inside and external sales can accurately capture those activities conducted in their organization.
2. All qualified domestic leads will be worked and transitioned to the relevant account sales executives on the domestic sales force. The ASE for the particular region is *responsible* for engaging the qualified lead and "pushing" to strategic accounts as appropriate.

SALES PROCESS DEFINITION

Sales Stage	Milestones
Target	Fortune 1000 Financial Intuitions, 500 largest Healthcare, Lead generation campaigns and inbound calls
Suspects	Customers to assess interest, customer's interest identified
Prospects	Interest verified by more than one buying influencers, paid identified
Qualified Prospects	All decision makers identified, process identified, verified budged, sponsors identified, plan to buy one or more of our features
Evaluation Prospects	Meet with all key decision makers, verified pain and decision process, value proposition developed reviewed and agreed to by all key decision makers, Committed to evaluation decision within 30 days, Required activities for decision identified and scheduled.
Evaluation Partners	All activities required for decision complete, evaluation agreement; signed P.O., evaluation criteria identified and documented
Acceptance	Evaluation complete, contract approval verified, P.O. date committed, agreement signed

3.0 HIGH-LEVEL INSIDE SALES ADMIN. / MANAGEMENT

3.1 DAILY ROUTINE

The following activities will be conducted by each ISR daily:

1. Check e-mails and unfinished sales force tasks/callbacks from previous day
2. Check three-week outlook rolling appointment calendar w/ ASEs
3. Begin lead prioritization (see above)
4. Begin calling
5. Upon completion of initial prequalification call, enter into SF.com
6. Enter required information as a new lead in the LEADS database in SF.com (see below)
7. Notify field rep. of any appointments made (appropriate contact and qualifying information)
8. Task all uncontacted calls as "follow-up" calls in SF
9. Contact outside reps. to discuss progress ("fireside chat")
10. Send international leads out of LCD to international field
11. Complete literature fulfillment
12. Verify next day's tasks

3.2 INSIDE SALES LITERATURE FULFILLMENT

Inside sales literature fulfillment will be processed as follows:

- Literature fulfillment will be determined by Marketing— Packets
- A box of full literature packets will be distributed to each inside rep.
- Only Qualified Leads and Qualified Prospects will get full literature packets
- All other leads/prospects will be e-mailed PDF files with quotes

- Timely and accurate maintenance via database that includes updated e-mail addresses

3.3 LEAD FULFILLMENT, ENGAGEMENT, AND HAND-OFF:

- See High-Level and Detailed Inside Sales Process Flows/ Walkthrough in Sections 2.1, 2.2, 2.5, and 2.6.

3.4 LEVERAGING EACH CALL

- Utilize custom Probing Questions and Marketing tagline introductions
- Leave a voice mail on the first contact, which leads them to review the Web site / snapshot of what the (insert your company name here) Product/Service suite/Practices has to offer—unique.
- Leave task/note in SF.com indicating contact info, or whether a voice mail was left.
- Probing and identifying the right contact/decision-maker within target is valuable.
  - Track your activity daily and submit accurate and timely status reports as required.

4.0 Proposed SalesForce.com Changes (to "Lead Form")

The table below summarized the proposed changes required in SF.com ("Lead Form") to execute the details described in Sections 2 and 3 above. There are no changes to the Accounts, Contacts, or Opportunities forms. These forms should continue to function as they were pre-inside sales organization establishment.

ITEM #

1   Lead source: Lead source:

Lead source:	Lead source:
• Inside Sales	• ISR (Inside Sales Representative)
• Advertisement	• ASE (Account Sales Executives)
• Employee Referral	• Ad – (example: *Red Herring*)
• External Referral	• DM – (example: 12/05/YR)
• Online Campaign	• OC – (example: 12/05/ YR)
• Partner	• TS – (example: N+I Spring YR)
• Prospecting/Cold Call	• Channel Partner
• Public Relations	• Strategic Partner
• Seminar—Internal	• Employee Referral
• Seminar—Partner	• Customer Referral
• Trade Show	• Web Site
• Web	
• Word of Mouth	
• Other	

2   Model:
- Product Name
- Business Unit Service

3   Rating:
- Target List
- Suspect
- Prospect
- Qualified Prospect
- Evaluation Prospect
- Customer E/Prospect

(Insert your company name here) Technologies Inside Sales—Baseline Script

LINE #	SCRIPT	NOTE
Line 1	Good morning / afternoon, (prospect's name), my name is (your name) with (insert your company name here) Technologies in Silicon Valley, California. How are you today?	Greeting
Line 2	Are you the appropriate contact to discuss _____ solutions for your company's Web infrastructure?—If *no*, record appropriate contact info.	Right Contact
Line 3	The purpose of my call today is to briefly whet your appetite and introduce (insert your company name here) Technologies and an exciting new product we're launching, as well as to identify any of your current or expected pains / needs.	Introduction
Line 4	Have you heard of (insert your company name here) Technologies? We built the company initially on our family of _____ products (insert product name here) and we've just announced the launch of _____ business services. Because of the truly next-generation approach taken by our company _____ takes a quantum leap forward in end-to-end solutions.	Teaser

Line 5   Key benefits: Meat

> • Strong X
>   - X
>   - X
>   - X
>   Low TCO

In a nutshell, the (insert your company name here) (insert product name here) delivers high performance _____ _____.

Line 6   Does this sound like something you'd be   Hook
interested in? Do you have employees/partners that _____? Do you currently have _____ in place? If so what?

TAKEAWAYS

1. Interest identified (product or business unit services, pricing, etc.)
2. Appropriate contact (name, title, telephone, e-mail address); additional contacts/decision-makers
3. Current/expected pains/needs
4. Existing security/IT/networking infrastructure, planned expansion, and timing
5. Process

(INSERT YOUR COMPANY NAME HERE) COLLATERAL STATUS AT A GLANCE

Project Name:
Date Assigned:
Production Group: Marketing
Target End Date:
Primary Marketing Contact:
Primary Sales Contact:
Plan Authorship and Approval;
Approval Date: (m/d/yy)
Plan Authored by: (Name(s))
Plan Approved by: (m/d/yy)
Final Deliverable Received:
_____ (Sales Signature) _____ (Mktg. Signature)

Project Goals—Overall goal/Objective of this collateral

-
-

Background Situation Analysis—Current situation from which the document will arise from

-
-

Audience—Who we want to reach, target market. Please include detailed description

-
-

Messages—List the key messages to be delivered in this collateral

-
-

Assets—Briefly list the people, channel and other assets that we can use

-
-

What are the main messages for this copy?

-
-

Specific services, products, technology standards that we need to include

-
-

Important facts that need to be included in collateral

-
-

Executable guidelines

-
-

What kind of illustrations can be used?

-
-

Is their special paper that this needs to be printed on? Please explain

-
-

(INSERT YOUR COMPANY NAME HERE) COLLATERAL AT A GLANCE— ACTION PLAN TEMPLATE

Current Phase of Project: _____
_____
_____

Describe Goal(s)/Missing: _____
_____
_____

Editor's Notes: _____
_____

Action Step/ Revision Number	Resources Needed	Resources Available	Person(s) Responsible	Others to Involve to Complete Action Step	Time Line / Dates of completion
yy/m/d rev #					

Marketing Materials

- **Executive Questionnaire** (Templates)
- **Positioning Outline** (Templates)
- **A Unified Communications Approach** (Templates)
- **Brand Strategy and Launch Plan** (Templates)

MARCOM TEAM PROCESS FLOW

(Designation of teams; assignment of responsibilities)

Activity Flow	Responsible Team (*= To take Action)
1. Determine Budget Location	PL / MC
2. Complete Project Definition or Request Funds Transfer	PL / MC (local budget) PM
3. Develop Creative Platform/Project Briefing	MC
4. Determine PR Involvement/PR Strategy	PM / PR / PL

5. Schedule Preproduction Meeting
   a. Complete Worksheets
     1) Choose response mechanism
     2) Identify pieces (may include data sheet)
   b. Determine use of various media options
     3) Advertisements
     4) WWW
     5) Information CD ROM (internal)
     6) Channel marketing
	PM / MC
	
	PM / MC

6. Complete Input Form	PL/PM
7. Quotes from Vendors (may need various options)	MC
8. Select Vendor	MC
9. Initiate Purchase Req./: Required on vendor quote: - Budget number, ship-to location with quantity, delivery date	MC (local budget)
10. Initiate Purchase Req.	PM (cc of request to MC)
11. Shipping Instructions to Vendor	
12. Production	MC

13. Project Status and Approvals
  ✓ Project status meeting (weekly)
  ✓ Production proof approvals (ongoing)
  ✓ Formal approval cycle (s) per Marcom process
  ✓ Marcom, marketing, legal
	PM / MC
	MC
	PM

14. Sign off Form	PM / MC / PM / L
15. Measurement/Results/Feedback	PM / MC
16. Close Out Production Folder After Receipt	MC

PM = Product Manager; MC = Marcom, A = Agency, PL = Product Line Manager
CM = Channel Marketing, S = Sales, M = Marketing, L = Legal

TRADE SHOW FLOW

Marcom Process:

Goal: Develop an efficient trade show management and execution process by assigning responsibilities to the appropriate people according to job functions such as: program manager, trade show coordinator, manager marketing communications, public relations (PR), and production manager.

Trade Show Elements	Responsible
Budget Management	Program Manager
Technical Papers/Session Chairperson	Product Marketing with Program Manager and PR
Source Worksheet (put in place)	Program Manager to Direct Marketing Manager
Advertising/Promotion	
✓ Program listing/product listing	Program Manager with Product Marketing
✓ Press meetings/editorial contact/press kits	PR (keep program manager informed)
✓ Hospitality suite (customer and/or press)	Program Manager and/or PR with T S Coordinator
✓ Show event sponsorship	Program Manager with Production Mgr.
Primary Messages/Graphics/Signage	
✓ Messages/creative direction	Product Marketing with Program Manager
	Production Mgr. (Produce graphics/signage)
	T S Coordinator (ship graphics/signage to booth)
Demos/Display at Booth	
✓ Develop plan/set creative direction	Product Marketing with Program Manager (decide) Production Mgr. (If production required) T S Coordinator (ship to booth)

Giveaways
   ✓   Develop plan/set creative
          direction
	Program Manager
	Production Mgr. (Produce)
	T S Coordinator (ship to booth)

Literature for Booth (minimum quantities)	Program Manger (decide) T S Coordinator (order and ship)
Booth	
✓ On-site management of booth	Program Manager and/or TS Coordinator
✓ Show services (electrical, phones, etc.)	T S Coordinator (with input from Program Manager)
✓ Product marketing attendees names	Program Manager to T S Coordinator
✓ Booth information and booth schedule	T S Coordinator: (contact field sales/FAEs for names, integrate product marketing names, develop schedule; distribute information memo with final booth schedule)
✓ Show passes (free)	T S Coordinator (order; distribute to mktg. and sales)
✓ Badges	T S Coordinator (order for "at show" pickup)
✓ Hotel (information on selected show hotels)	T S Coordinator to Prog. Manager to Product Mktg.
Leads from Trade Show	Prog. Manager/TS Coor. to Direct Marketing Mgr.
Galley of Leads for Marketing to Edit/ Review	Direct Marketing Mgr. to Program Manger to Mktg.
Return Edited Galley of Leads	Mktg. to Program Mgr to Direct Marketing Mgr
Measurement: Database/Response Report	Direct Marketing Mgr to Program Mgr & Mktg.

Permission Marketing Overview

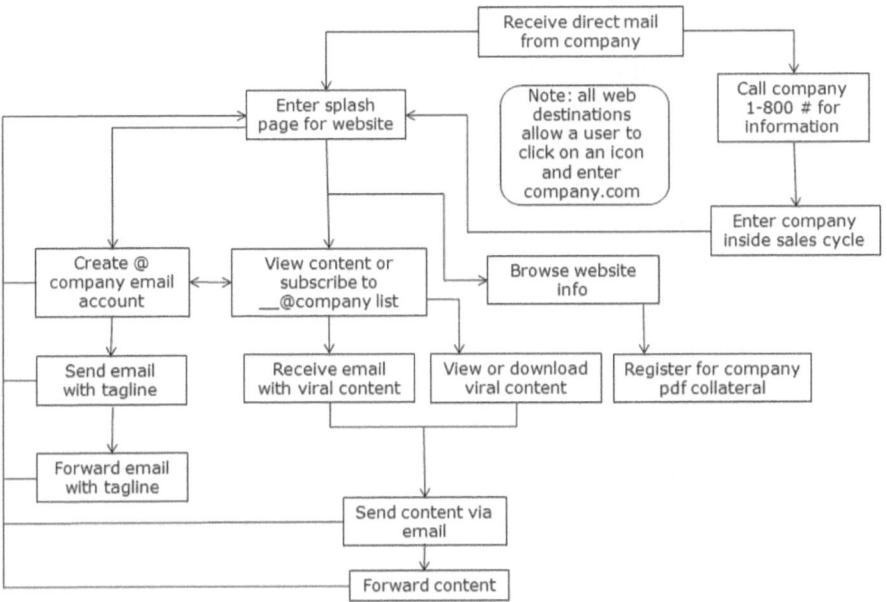

MARKETING   Date sent out: _____

COMMUNICATIONS   Date due back: _____

Sign-Off Sheet   This is approval cycle number: _____

Your approval is required on the attached material.
Please review, make changes or corrections, or sign off as is.
Note the date this form is due back to us.

Item for sign-off: _____

At development/production stage: _____

For division: _____

Purpose/use: _____

Audience: _____

Distribution: _____

Production specs: _____

Quantity to print: _____

Signatures required to release this piece to the next stage:

COO: _____ Date: _____

Director of Sales: _____ Date: _____
Product Manager: _____ Date: _____

Marketing: _____ Date: _____

Legal Counsel: _____ Date: _____

Please sign or initial by your name; be sure to include the date you sign:

- Approved as is. - Approved with changes noted. - Not approved.

Return to: Ext:

Please write comments on the back of this sheet if necessary. Thanks

Fax to: (Insert company name here)
                  Street, City, State Zip Code
                  Attn: Admin. of Inside Sales   Date:
                  Fax no: 000-000-0000

MARKETING MATERIALS ORDER FORM FOR SALES

- Please find below a list of (insert company name here) marketing support materials available to (insert company name here) sales team.
- Quantities are limited.

Promotional Items	Quantity	Purpose & Customers
Caps		
T-Shirts		
TOTAL		

Collaterals	Quantity	Purpose and Customers
Datasheet		
Full Line Brochure		
Customer Support Brochure		
Brochure XYZ		
Banners		
Press Kits		
Sales Binder		
VAR Binder		
Corporate Letterhead		
Corporate Envelope		
Corporate Folder		
TOTAL		

(Insert company name here) Salesperson:
(Insert company name here) Inside Sales:
Shipment Method/ Requested Arrival Date:
Sales Signature: Date:

Sales Director/ VP Approval: Date:
Marketing Approval: Date:

Reason for Rejection (if applicable):
- Request submitted without (insert company name here) regional sales director / VP of sales approval
- Request submitted without marketing approval
- Others (explanation):

QUALITY ASSURANCE

Strategy

Templates
- QA Forms and Design
- Sieve Overview

STRATEGY

(Insert your company name here) is renowned for quality. As you also know, our methods of distribution and selling will always position (insert your company name here) as a high-priced high value-added dealer. When a person purchases a $100,000+ Bentley or Ferrari, people do not mind paying for quality. On that same note, such a product and service must reflect that quality.

Please review the attached proposed "Quality Assurance" package. I would like this package to be included in all of our lead Halo products master cartons for the beginning and later carried out to all products/equipment. It would also be an integral part of the sales force day-to-day sales tools to show prospective and existing customers. If all (insert your company name here) business units adapt this package, the individual costs per units will go down.

Contents of Quality Assurance Package:

- Quality Assurance Presentation Folder (white chrome coat stock with gold-foil lettering.
- Thanks from (insert your company name here)
  - Photograph of everyone in manufacturing facility
- (Insert your company name here) ESP Flyer
- Warranty Response Card
- (Insert your company name here) Brochure
- Division Product Line Brochures

Quality Assurance Follow-Up Letter

- Three weeks after receiving the product warranty response card from the customer, we will send a quality assurance follow-up letter.

End of Warranty Letter

- One month before customers warranty expires, division will send letter with "Service Coupon."

QA FORMS
CUSTOMER SATISFACTION FORM

(Insert your company name here)
Address
Suite _00
City, State Zip-Code

Dear (insert your company name here) customer,

Our records show your _____ is almost out of warranty. You can be assured that all of us at (insert your company name here) are determined to do everything we can to keep your equipment in peak operating condition. We think in partnership terms.

One phase of this effort, to make sure that our customers are fully satisfied, is the coupon at the bottom of this letter. It details some of the special offers on service available to our customers. You have up to one year to redeem the coupon.

If you have not already done so, please contact our (insert city) Customer Service Centers for help in any way that we can provide.

Sincerely;

First-Name Last-Name
Manager, Customer Services

PLEASE CUT ALONE THE DOTTED LINE

(Insert Your Company Name Here)

SERVICE COUPON

$_ _.00 Discount

Authorized Signature

Valid at (Company Name)

Not Redeemable For Cash
Not Valid With Any Other Discounts
Expires 12/31/20__)

II. CONTENTS OF QUALITY ASSURANCE PACKAGE: (ILLUSTRATION)

Quality
Assurance
Packet

Thank You

Photograph

From (Insert Your
Company Here)

Warranty Card

Warranty Quality
Assurance
Follow Up Letter

From (Insert Your
Company Here)

Product
Brochure

CUSTOMER SATISFACTION FORM

(Insert your company name here)

Quality Assurance

Please help (insert your company name here) identify the areas of customer satisfaction and dissatisfaction with the (insert your company name here) installation process so that we will be able to identify areas for improvement. Thank you very much for your assistance.

Date distributed:		
Customer name:		
Customer number:		
Customer contact:		
Shipping address:		
Options:		
Platform (hardware):	O/S:	
Installer Users:		
Date installed:		
___Yes	___No	Did we send the software to the correct person and address? If not, please indicate the corrections above.
___Yes	___No	Do you prefer another media for software?
___Yes	___No	Will you also be a user of this software?
___Yes	___No	Do you have system manager knowledge?
___Yes	___No	Did you need system manager assistance?
___Yes	___No	Have you installed (insert your company name here) software before?
___Yes	___No	Have you ever used (insert your company name here) software before?
		What is the average user's level of experience on the computer/video system that (insert your company name here) is running on? ____ none ____ some ____ good ____ expert
___Yes	___No	Do you feel that you should be able to install (insert your company name here) software on your system without being a system expert?
___Yes	___No	Do you feel a user should be able to run this software with little knowledge of the computer/video system is running on?
___Yes	___No	Did you use the Installation Guide document?
___Yes	___No	Would you have preferred to get the Installation Guide ahead of time?
___Yes	___No	Was the Installation Guide document adequate?
___Yes	___No	What else would have been helpful? (Place answer on reverse side)

___Yes	___No	Were you involved in evaluating the hardware/software for purchase?
___Yes	___No	Were you involved in placing the order with (insert your company name here) sales?
___Yes	___No	Did you receive any contact or information from (insert your company name here) about installing this before receiving the shipment?
___Yes	___No	Did you require and/or receive assistance from someone at (insert your company name here) to help with the installation?
___Yes	___No	If you obtained assistance, was it easy to get?
___Yes	___No	Were you satisfied with the level of assistance provided?
___Yes	___No	Did you have to make any changes to your hardware/software before you could install and operate the system?
		Per the number of programs in your installation, do you feel the installation is (in disk space usage): ___ small ___ average ___ large ___ very large?
		Per the number of programs in your installation, do you feel the time required to complete installation was ____ acceptable or ____ too long?
		How long did the installation take? _____ hours _____ minutes
		What was the system/CPU used during installation? _____ ____
___Yes	___No	During the (insert your company name here) installation, did this CPU have to compete with other users/programs sharing that system's resources?

*Please write additional comments here, on the back, or on another sheet.

CUSTOMER RETENTION

Templates
- Frequent Users Club
- Volume Incentive Program

(INSERT YOUR COMPANY NAME HERE) "USERS CLUB"

DON'T MISS OUT ON THE FUN AND EXCITEMENT...

JOIN THE NEW (INSERT YOUR COMPANY NAME HERE) "USERS CLUB" TODAY!

We have received letters from (INSERT YOUR COMPANY NAME HERE) customers who wanted to hear more about new and existing products and product applications on a regular basis. As a result, we've formed the new (INSERT YOUR COMPANY NAME HERE) "Users Club."

We are very pleased to invite you to become a member of this select group of broadcast/professional video industry enthusiasts; this club is especially for you!

RECEIVE AN EXCLUSIVE "Users Club" MEMBERSHIP KIT!

- Official (INSERT YOUR COMPANY NAME HERE) T-shirt
- Official Membership Card
- Fact-filled Newsletter
- New Products Announcements
- (INSERT YOUR COMPANY NAME HERE) Fun Book
- And more!

"USERS CLUB" NEWSLETTER: YOUR KEY TO VALUABLE INFORMATION.

The "Users Club" newsletter will give you the latest information about new products, and provide you with exclusive inside stories on product applications. Each issue of the newsletter will feature articles on (INSERT YOUR COMPANY NAME HERE) products from the past, present, and future! You will learn special features about the latest product—straight from our Technical Support and Customer Service groups.

PREMIUMS

The "Users Club" will offer merchandise for purchase by members— t-shirts, pens, posters, and more. The newsletter will also announce special contests and events with great prizes, available only to you as a member of this exclusive club.

ACT NOW AND RECEIVE AN EARLY BIRD BONUS GIFT!

As a special way of saying thanks, all memberships will receive a bonus gift with the membership kit; a classic (INSERT YOUR COMPANY NAME HERE) t-shirt will be selected as your special bonus gift.

If you have friends who may also be interested, please pass along this flyer to them.

To join, complete the Membership form on the following page.

(Don't forget to send it with the (INSERT YOUR COMPANY NAME HERE) response card)

OFFICIAL (INSERT YOUR COMPANY NAME HERE) "USERS CLUB" MEMBERSHIP APPLICATION FORM

PLEASE ENROLL ME AS A ONE-YEAR MEMBER OF THE OFFICIAL (INSERT YOUR COMPANY NAME HERE) "USERS CLUB" FOR THE ANNUAL MEMBERSHIP FEE OF $5.00.* SEND CHECK OR MONEY ORDERS ONLY (NO CASH) TO:

"Users Club"
(INSERT YOUR COMPANY NAME HERE)
Company Street Address
City, State Zip Code

(Please print)

_____
Name

_____
Address

_____
City   State   Zip Code

_____
Names of your favorite manufacture

Please indicate your T-shirt size:

Adult: sm   med   lrg   x-lrg

*Allow 6-8 weeks for delivery of membership kit.

(INSERT YOUR COMPANY NAME HERE)
FREQUENT BUYER CLUB

(INSERT YOUR COMPANY NAME HERE)
Frequent Buyer Club
Date

Name
Company
Address
City, State Zip code

Dear Mr. X. X:

Today we are proud to bring to you the (INSERT YOUR COMPANY NAME HERE) Frequent Buyer Club program.

- Plateau prizes
- "Free Goods" promotions
- New, early payment incentive terms
- "Bonus" coupons earned for customer referrals.
- "Bonus" coupons for conducting (INSERT YOUR COMPANY NAME HERE) open house

The following page describes our program in detail. And you're already one step out of the starting gate right now. We've enclosed a "complimentary" entry for you that entitles you to one entry in Plateau Level <u>A</u> (you only need four more coupons to make it) and if you conduct an (INSERT YOUR COMPANY NAME HERE) Products Open House at your facility you receive an additional free coupon (you only need three more to make it) and one entry in the Grand Prize drawing to be held on January 6, 20__.

Our Frequent Buyer Club program lets you earn "BONUS" coupons during the year by recommending customers to us and for putting the "(INSERT YOUR COMPANY NAME HERE)" in any of your company's advertisements (Up to Five (5) advertisements during promotion. Each "BONUS" coupon is a dual purpose coupon: (1)

another entry in the Grand Prize drawing, and (2) another coupon entry in the Plateau Prize segment of our program.

Let's face it—we want to show our products to you and your staff, who will tell others. At the same time, it will certainly be worth your efforts. Start today and your first prize could arrive before Christmas!

Sincerely,

(INSERT YOUR COMPANY NAME HERE)
FREQUENT BUYER CLUB

Date

Name
Company
Address
City, State Zip code

Dear Mr. X. X:

Congratulations! You've reached the first plateau in the (INSERT YOUR COMPANY NAME HERE) Frequent Buyer Club. So now it's "decision time!"

Should you now order Plateau Prize <u>A</u>, the _____? <u>Or</u>, should you opt to move onward and upward during the program and accumulate your coupons toward a more valuable prize in a higher plateau?

I'm glad the choice is <u>yours</u>! Whatever your decision, we'll support you all the way.

An official order form is enclosed, which you should complete and send in to (INSERT YOUR COMPANY NAME HERE) for handling, if you choose to order Plateau Prize <u>A</u>. Please allow four to six weeks for delivery.

Keep up your solid performance for (INSERT YOUR COMPANY NAME HERE) products, and remember, "Bonus" coupons can be earned for recommending customers to use (INSERT YOUR COMPANY NAME HERE) for (INSERT YOUR COMPANY NAME HERE)/ Customer advertisements. It will pay off for all of us!

Sincerely,

(INSERT YOUR COMPANY NAME HERE)
FREQUENT BUYER CLUB

Date

Name
Company
Address
City, State Zip code

Dear Mr. X. X:

Your facility continues to purchase (INSERT YOUR COMPANY NAME HERE) product. You've now reached the second plateau in the (INSERT YOUR COMPANY NAME HERE) "Frequent Buyer Club" program. Time again to think about prize selection.

Should you now order Plateau Prize <u>B</u>, the _____? <u>Or</u>, should you think about ordering two Plateau A prizes? Or, should you opt to move onward and upward during the program and bank your hours toward a more valuable prize in a higher plateau?

Decisions!   Decisions!   Decisions!

An official order form is enclosed, which you should complete and send to X for handling, if you choose to order plateau prizes now. Please allow four to six weeks for delivery.

I want to personally thank you for your support of (INSERT YOUR COMPANY NAME HERE) products, and remember, "Bonus" coupons can be earned for recommending new customers to use (INSERT YOUR COMPANY NAME HERE) and for (INSERT YOUR COMPANY NAME HERE)/Customer advertisements.

Sincerely,

OFFICIAL COUPON
No. 0001

(INSERT YOUR COMPANY NAME HERE)
Frequent Buyer Club

NAME OF COMPANY

YOUR NAME: PHONE:

ADDRESS:

CITY: STATE: ZIP:

Approved by (INSERT YOUR COMPANY NAME HERE) District Manager

DUAL PURPOSE COUPON

1. This coupon is valid for the above named authorized by (INSERT YOUR COMPANY NAME HERE) Dealer toward earning the prizes specified in the "plateau levels" portion of the by (INSERT YOUR COMPANY NAME HERE) Frequent Buyer Club program, in accordance with the Official Rules and Regulations. Coupon must be redeemed by no later than December 31, 20__. Void after that date.

2. ALSO, this coupon officially enters the (INSERT YOUR COMPANY NAME HERE) Frequent Buyer Club member into the drawing for Grand Prize winners. Drawing will be made January 5, 20__ by (INSERT YOUR COMPANY NAME HERE). Frequent Buyer Club member need not be present to win.

OFFICIAL COUPON
No. 0002

(INSERT YOUR COMPANY NAME HERE)
Frequent Buyer Club

NAME OF COMPANY

YOUR NAMEPHONE

ADDRESS

CITY   STATE   ZIP

Approved by (INSERT YOUR COMPANY NAME HERE) District Manager

DUAL PURPOSE COUPON

1. This coupon is valid for the above named (INSERT YOUR COMPANY NAME HERE) customer toward earning the prizes specified in the "plateau levels" portion of the (INSERT YOUR COMPANY NAME HERE) Frequent Buyer Club program, in accordance with the Official Rules and Regulations. Coupon must be redeemed by no later than December 31, 20__. Void after that date.

2. ALSO, this coupon officially enters the (INSERT YOUR COMPANY NAME HERE) Frequent Buyer Club member into the drawing for Grand Prize winners. Drawing will be made January 5, 20__ by (INSERT YOUR COMPANY NAME HERE). Frequent Buyer Club member need not be present to win.

V.I.P.—VOLUME INCENTIVE PROGRAM AGREEMENT

1. Period:	One Year Beginning:	Ending:		
2. Products:	Product A Product B Product C Product D Product E			
3. Prices:	The pricing charged by (insert your company here) to for the products shall be those established by (insert your company here) from time to time for its VIP Volume Incentive Program.			
4. Rebates:	Product Line A	Product Line B	Product Line C	Systems Design & Installations
	Over $ 300K - 1%	Over $ 1.0 M - 1%	Over $ 750K - 1%	Over $1.0 M - 1%
	Over $ 400K - 2%	Over $ 1.5 M - 2%	Over $ 1M - 2%	Over $1.5 M - 2%
	Over $ 500K - 3%	Over $ 2.0 M - 3%		Over $2.0 M - 3%
	Over $ 600K - 4%	Over $ 2.5 M - 4%		Over $2.5 M - 4%
	Over $ 700K - 5%	Over $ 3.0 M - 5%		Over $3.0 M - 5%
5. Terms and Conditions:	Are those specified herein for this program, and those generally listed in the (insert your company here) standard terms and conditions on the reverse of our purchase orders.			
6. Delivery:	(Insert your company here) shall endeavor to ship accepted orders within a reasonable time.			

Parts, Accessories, N.R.E.: Non-Recovery Engineering Expenses, Extended Warranty, and Restocking Charges are not included in rebate program. Rebates are inclusive on product shipped, billed, and paid in full during this agreement, and are based on the Calendar Monthly Computer Run sales accomplishment reports. Any returned equipment or canceled purchased orders after rebate credit memorandum is given will be subject to bill back.

Rebates will be credited for the plateau reached in the form of a credit memorandum at the end of this agreement time period. Should any questions arise; the Calendar Monthly Computer Run will be the official document by which rebates are determined.

Participation in this program is limited to (insert your company here) having a signed VIP Volume Incentive Program Agreement on file with (insert your company here) headquarter.

Typed Name and Title of:
Signatory:
(Insert your company here) Signatory:

INSTRUCTIONS FOR COMPLETING
Volume Incentive Program

1. Sign the attached agreement
2. Type signatory name, title, and date
3. Keep copy for your file

Send original to (insert your company here) Att: Mr/Ms _____, (Insert your mailing address here)

4. (Insert your company here) will sign and complete the agreement and return it to you.
5. Each time you submit a purchase order, please record it. The local _____ Sales Office and our computer tab run will also have records of your purchase.

SUMMARY

My primary goal has been to provide an actionable resource MAP, to focus on the major initiatives facing marketing professionals and to help harmonize the objectives and resources of an organization. This book presents a framework of recurrent marketing challenges.

As an industry innovator and achiever, I have drawn from personal experience, observations, and opinions.

I have moved past conventional approaches and explored the new problems that face companies and the new concepts needed to deal effectively with these problems. Marketing control is the natural continuation of marketing planning, organization, and implementation. Systematic short-run and long-run plans will improve the organization's overall marketing efficacy.

By facing the problems head-on and accurately citing solutions, I have sought to make this book a must-read for marketing business leaders.

By applying marketing cross-disciplines to a wide range of relevance from enterprises, consumer markets, services, small companies as well as large ones, nonprofit organizations as well as for-profit companies, it provides balanced and comprehensive coverage. The book avoids uneven coverage of strategies, tactics, or guidance. It covers all other topics about which marketing managers need some diversified knowledge.

You hold in your hands numerous comprehensive marketing action plans for immediate implementation for your business and marketing needs.

I invite you to contact me if you have any questions, comments, or suggestions. I can be reached at <u>morgan@morganrees.com</u>.

About the Author

Morgan Rees is a proven executive with international and domestic marketing, branding, and sales experience in the consumer and business-to-business industries. He built a reputation on consistently driving profitable growth and market success by focusing on market share, brand awareness, and building the business bottom line for such renowned start-ups and established brands as Citrix Online, Philips Electronics, Norelco, Marantz, Magnavox, Netgear, and Honeywell.

Morgan has a perfect blend of marketing experience, having worked on both the client and advertising agency side of business early in his career with companies like Toyota, Oldsmobile, Swim 'n Sport and Red Lobster.

Combination of online and offline marketing expertise:

- Developed strategies for a full spectrum of traditional offline communications, such as messaging, press relations, analyst relations, speaking engagements, presentations, white papers, case studies, tradeshows, direct-response campaigns, advertising (mobile, print, radio, and television), etc.
- Built online strategies and campaigns including a blend of Web sites, microsites, interactive, SEM, SEO, e-mail, banner, affiliate, direct response, ecommerce, social networking, electronic collateral, Web site management, webinars, flash movies, and interactive content.

- Created and maintained management procedures and best practices.

Earned reputation as a producer who has:

- Launched Philips brand into the United States—created consumer branding market awareness where none existed.
- Raised $24 million in VC funding—well versed in start-up investor relations.
- Developed/implemented branding strategies for Citrix Online, Philips, Norelco, Marantz, Magnavox, Netgear, Honeywell, Oldsmobile, Toyota, Swim 'n Sport, and Red Lobster.
- Collaborated on global product launches involving GoToMyPC, GoToMyWebinar, GoToMyMeeting, GoToAssist, GoToAssistExpress, Wi-Fi, GPS, CD-R/RW, DVD, Plasma Flat-TV, LCD-Display, MP3, cell phone/pagers, USB, and TiVo.
- Managed relationships with key online affiliates and consumer electronics retail partners.
- Team effort grew revenue from $100 million to $260 million, seized market share. (Data is from public Citrix annual reports and 10K.)
- Turned around companies with little-to-no momentum: Prior to joining Netgear, the company had been hemorrhaging sales for several years. Accomplished changes that reversed that trend and increased Netgear's sales and margins.
- Helped grow Philips Electronics Components division from start-up to a multi-one-hundred-million-dollar business.
- Led efforts that doubled revenues of two Honeywell business units.
- Increased sales from zero to $100 million in three years for Honeywell start-up.

A facility member of Florida International University and the author of numerous merketing-related articles in trade magazines.